C000050785

This series concentrates upon the basics of the English Language.

The activities are straightforward, brief and to the point. They offer repetition and progression providing a firm grounding in the language.

Each book covers: Writing
                      Spelling
                      Grammar
                      Comprehension

How To Get The Best Out Of This Book

National Curriculum
Key Stage 2 covers a period when children are required to absorb a wide range of information and develop and master many skills. This book addresses the end of Key Stage 2. The content covers:

Reading for Understanding
A range of short stories and texts with comprehension questions.

Grammar and Punctuation
The basics are covered in a range of short exercises.

Kinds of Writing
Children are encouraged to develop styles of both narrative (story telling) and writing for a purpose.

Spelling
Phonics are used to help develop and reinforce spelling skills.

Age Range
This book is aimed at the average Year 6 (age10/11) child. Book 1 covers age 7/8, Book 2 age 8/9 and Book 3 age 9/10.

How To Use The Book
Each book contains more than you are likely to need before progressing to the next book, be selective. Concentrate upon one aspect (e.g. spelling) and do not use every exercise unless your child has difficulty.

This edition prepared, 1993.
© Folens Publishers Ltd. Dunstable. Dublin.

Contents

New Treasury of English 4

New Treasury of English is a core scheme that aims to introduce children to the salient features of English grammar. The series develops their ability to comprehend written passages and utilises both grammar and comprehension in a series of relevant and structured exercises. The passages have been carefully chosen to give a wide variety of interesting material drawn from both fact and fiction.

How the books are constructed

Comprehension. The passages are of varying length and complexity. The child is asked a series of questions. In some cases the answers are explicit in the passage while in others they are implicit. Some questions go beyond the confines of the passage and draw on the pupil's more general experience and skills. In addition there are a number of exercises that are designed specifically to encourage children to look for meaning in writing rather than merely to decode words.

Grammar. The only grammar introduced is that which will enhance the child's style of writing and speech. Grammar is not treated as an end in itself; technical names for parts of speech, for example, are not used at this level. Each point is introduced by a brief explanation and followed by several sets of reinforcement and consolidation exercises.

Written style. In each book there are several sections that aim to broaden and develop pupil's written style. These vary from drawing attention to over-used words and suggesting alternatives to extending sentence construction. In this book we concentrate on broadening the child's written vocabulary through a series of structured exercises.

How to use these books

Each book contains more work than you are likely to need in one school year. You will probably need to be selective by either concentrating on one particular aspect of the book, say grammar or style or by deciding that it is not necessary for the pupils to complete every exercise

The comprehension passages, in particular, lend themselves to a number of differing approaches. They can certainly be used by the individual child but they can also be used by groups of children, thus providing the basis for useful discussion. They could also be used as completely oral exercises. By starting with some of the shorter passages you could provide a progressive course in listening skills.

The observation of nature and the passage of the seasons provide the major linking theme throughout the book and you may find it useful to use this material to stimulate direct observational work of the children's own environment. Perhaps they could keep an illustrated nature diary.

Whatever you decide to do, you will find that **New Treasury of English,** as well as providing a core scheme, enables you, the teacher, to achieve a high degree of flexibility of approach

Fact File

(A) Fill in the blank spaces.

My name is .... and I am .... years old.
I live at ....
I have .... hair and .... eyes.
I am .... tall and weigh ....
There are .... people in my family.
Their names are ....
....
The youngest in the family is ....
I attend .... (school).
My teacher's name is ....
There are .... pupils in my class.

My best friends.	My favourite food.
1.	1. ....
2.	2. ....
3.	3. ....

My favourite games.	My favourite T.V. programme.
1.	1. ....
2.	2. ....
3.	3. ....

My neighbourhood.

(B) Describe your neighbourhood under these headings.

1. Its location, whether in the city, town or country.
2. Interesting facts you know about your area.
3. Play areas.
4. Where you shop.
5. Neighbours.
6. People who work in your area.
7. Improvements you would like to see.

My House.

(C) Draw a picture of your house.

Jenny The Jennet

A great roar filled the Big Top when Cheeky the Clown led out the *bucking* jennet. The ringmaster, dressed in his corduroy pants, red swallow-tail coat and hard hat, offered a prize of ten pounds to any rider who could ride the *vicious* jennet twice round the ring.

Big Tom Brown was first to step in to the *arena*. Tom fancied himself as a rider and liked to ride bareback. Indeed, he succeeded in completing one lap of the course. Just as he was about to gallop around the ring for the second time, Cheeky the Clown burst a big balloon. The terrified jennet kicked his hind legs in the air and sent his rider flying across the centre of the ring. The audience laughed when Tom landed with a *thud* in a cloud of sawdust.

Next, a brave country boy *ventured* into the ring and mounted the bucking jennet. In the twinkling of an eye, the helpless rider was left sitting on the ground.

Many other *plucky* boys tried their luck, but all in vain. The audience cheered wildly when one of the clowns grabbed the jennet's tail and was dragged out of the ring.

Dictionary work: Find out the meaning of: buck; arena; vicious; thud; venture; plucky. Write each word in a sentence of your own.

Questions

1. How were the ten pounds to be won?
2. Who liked to ride bareback?
3. What terrified the jennet?
4. What happened to Tom Brown at the start of his second round of the ring?
5. How was the clown dragged out of the ring?
6. Write a few sentences to describe how you entered the ring and won the ten pounds.

The Full Stop

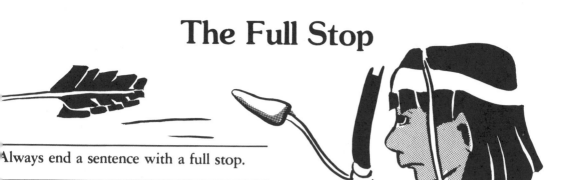

Always end a sentence with a full stop.

A) Write out these sentences, putting in the capital letters and full stops.

1. my friend has a bow and arrow
2. we saw a cowboy film
3. the chief smoked a peace-pipe
4. she lived with her husband in a large wigwam
5. all the young braves danced around the campfire
6. they traded their guns for buffalo hides
7. a pony galloped into the army fort
8. there was a young warrior behind the rock
9. soon the witch doctor began praying for rain
10. the waggon-train was attacked

B) There are two sentences in each of the following. Write them out, putting in the capital letters and full stops.

1. mary called with her friend nora today i showed them my new pet rabbit
2. we had to stay inside all day i was delighted when the rain stopped
3. the outlaws stopped the coach and robbed the passengers everybody was terrified
4. the wolf called the frog and the bear they promised to help him
5. the shepherd watched over his flock the wolf did not dare come near
6. the rocket lifted off it was going on a long voyage into outer space
7. she worked long hours on the farm she had the finest herd of cattle in the land
8. a huge pirate stood on the deck his name was blackbeard
9. snow fell during the night when i awoke, i wanted to make a snowman
10. the summer morning was bright and fair we set out for the seaside

C) Write out this paragraph, putting in the capital letters and full stops.

long, long ago the indians had no fire the only fire in the world was kept by three ugly witches they hated the indian tribes the witches took turns at guarding their precious fire and nobody could even get a spark from it

Snowy, The Polar Bear
Comprehension

Snowy, the polar bear, lives in the frozen lands of the Arctic. The Eskimos call him 'Nanook''. The bear's short legs, long body and slender snout give the *impression* of a slow-moving animal. Do not be *deceived*. Though weighing over 700 kilograms, Snowy can travel at speeds of 48 kms per hour. He is so strong that a single blow of his mighty paw can break the neck of an ox.

Snowy is an expert diver and swimmer. You may meet him 160-300 kms out in the ocean, calmly riding along on a floating iceberg or swimming gracefully in the freezing waters. His thick layers of fat allow him to remain a long time in the cold waters.

You and I wear sunglasses to protect our eyes from the sun's rays. Snowy has special eyelids that *shield* his eyes from the glare of the snow and ice. The soles of his feet are padded with fur. This prevents him from slipping on the ice and packed snow.

Nothing pleases the polar bear more than a good meal of seal flesh. This huge white hunter of the Arctic follows the migrating seals as far south as the Gulf of the Saint Lawrence river in Canada. Sniffing the clear air he is able to pick up the scent of seal *blubber* as far away as 30 kilometres.

When Snowy finds a seal's breathing hole in the ice he is very happy. He sits patiently near the mouth of the hole with his paw raised and ready to strike. The moment the seal appears, the bear's mighty claws of steel come down. He seldom misses his target. The daring Eskimo hides behind a white screen and waits for the polar bear to make his prized kill before shooting him. The Eskimo sells the bear's valuable skin at the trading station and brings the meat home to his family.

The deadly killer whale is the bear's greatest enemy. In the water Snowy is no match for this huge sea mammal. He must also keep a sharp look out for his enemy, the walrus, who is bigger and stronger than he is. Sometimes the fearless polar bear will sneak up on a sleeping walrus and bash its head in with a block of frozen ice.

The female bear gives birth to one or two cubs in a deep cave or snow tunnel. The new-born cubs weigh less than a kilogram and are blind and naked. The devoted mother protects her young and feeds them throughout the long winter. They remain with her for about 2 years. During this time the female bear is very dangerous and will bravely defend her young against attack. When the young polar bears are strong enough they wander off to lead their own *solitary* lives in the land of snow and ice.

Clumsy he may be, slow and unhurried, yet we cannot but admire this huge bear, 2½ metres high, that lives in the frozen lands of the Arctic.

Dictionary work: Find out the meaning of: impression; deceived; shield; blubber; solitary; clumsy. Write each word in a sentence of your own.

Questions: Answer the questions in sentence-form where possible.

1. In what part of the world does Snowy live?
2. Why is he called the "white hunter"?
3. How is it shown that the polar bear has great strength?
4. Why does he not freeze in the Arctic waters?
5. What protection has he from the glare of the snow?
6. Why does Snowy not slip on the ice?
7. What is the bear's favourite food?
8. What enemies has the polar bear?
9. Where are the cubs born?
10. How does the Eskimo kill the polar bear?

Insert the correct word under its proper heading.

List: bear, herring, magpie, plaice, crane, seal, eagle, doe, trout, otter, mackerel, curlew, salmon, swift, ostrich, ferret, pike, weasel, cod, buzzard, perch, stork, polecat, mole, shark, boar, shrew, raven, rook, whiting.

Animal	Fish	Bird
....	....	....
....	....	....
....	....	....
....	....	....
....	....	....
....	....	....
....	....	....
....	....	....
....	....	....

Wild Animals
Creative Writing

e is a piece of descriptive writing by Marion. She uses her imagination to write an
resting paragraph about the polar bear in the picture.

first caught sight of the polar bear as she
ily glided by on a floating iceberg. Far off
stood motionless and erect like a marble
ie. Her fleecy white fur blended with the
te landscape. Now and again she flicked
her tongue and licked a few snowflakes.
iddenly the old bear tossed her head,
fed the cool crisp air and plunged into the
waters.

te an interesting description or story about each animal below.

st of helpful words are given.

phant

jest animal .... powerful trunk .... ivory tusks .... trumpets and ambles
.... lives in a herd.

mel

Arabian desert .... beast of burden .... strong and sturdy ....
ws dates, dried grasses and grain.

ger

k striped animal .... razor-sharp teeth .... hunts at night ....
rs and prowls.

11

Capital Letters

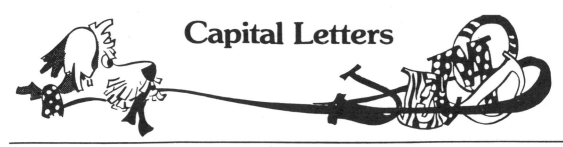

Capital letters are used for:

(i)	The start of a sentence.	My teacher is very intelligent.
(ii)	"I" when used on its own.	I was sick, so I went to bed.
(iii)	The names of people.	James and John White are twins.

(A) Insert the capital letters where needed in the following sentences.

1. at the end of every sentence there is a full stop.
2. she is older than i.
3. yesterday helen brady was absent from school.
4. i have a baby sister named jane.
5. pears and apples are delicious fruit.
6. peter and i went to the pictures together.
7. larry daly and michael rice are cousins.
8. susan and kathleen were at the circus.
9. every day the teacher gives us homework.
10. perhaps i can help you to paint the picture.
11. i have a friend whose name is julie.
12. i invited anne smith to my birthday party.
13. the teacher asked john to collect the books.
14. i helped helen and christopher to lift the heavy table.
15. my father spoke to doctor jones about my sore throat.

Capital letters are also used for:

(i)	The names of week days.	Sunday, Monday.
(ii)	The names of the months.	April, February.
(iii)	The names of special days and festivals.	Divali, Christmas Day.

(B) Insert the capital letters where needed in the following sentences.

1. Last wednesday the school team won the football final.
2. We have no school on good friday.
3. People all over the world celebrate christmas day.
4. November comes between october and december.
5. Muriel's mother made pancakes on shrove tuesday.
6. My summer holidays lasted from june to september.
7. We went to the seaside for the easter bank holiday.
8. In America the fourth of july is called independence day.
9. April the first is called 'fools' day.
10. Peter's best friend was born on new year's day.

Road Safety

Look at the following pictures and write:

1. What is wrong.
2. Why it is dangerous.
3. The correct way.

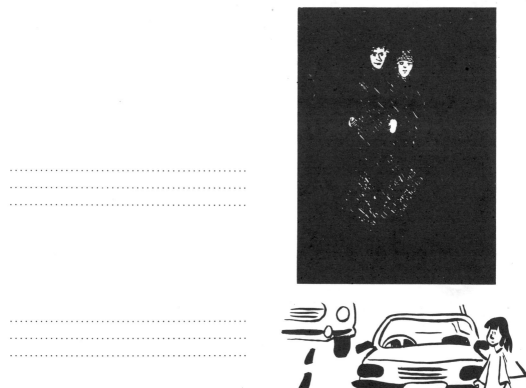

1. ....
2. ....
3. ....

1. ....
2. ....
3. ....

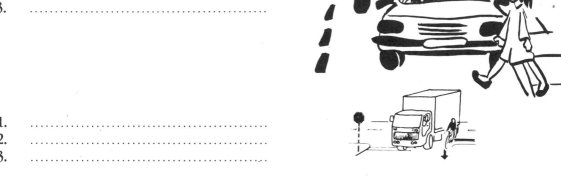

1. ....
2. ....
3. ....

1. ....
2. ....
3. ....

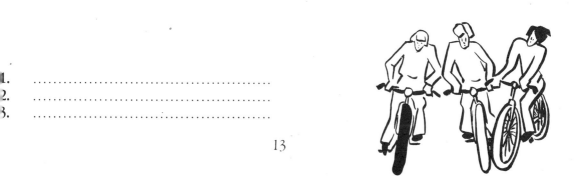

(A) Hand Signals: What do they mean?

1.

I am going to

....

2.

I am going to

....

3.

I am going to

....

(B) Road Signs: Write what each sign means.

1.

....

2.

....

3.

....

4.

....

5.

....

6.

....

7.

....

8.

....

9.

....

(C) Road Safety Quiz:

1. Name 5 safety features every bike should have.
2. What should you first do on entering a car?
3. When there is no footpath, on which side of the road should you walk?
4. Write the Safe Cross Code.
5. Why should one cycle slowly in wet weather?
6. How does a Garda signal traffic to stop?
7. What is the top colour on traffic lights?
8. Can you explain why so many accidents occur while children are crossing quiet roads?

Hero Of The Wild West

The most famous woman of the Wild West was Annie Oakley, who was born in a log cabin in Ohio, on August 13th, 1860. Her father died when she was only nine years of age, and her mother was left to support a large family of young children. In order to help her mother, Annie took to trapping wild animals and to hunting and shooting buffalo and deer. It was not long before she became a crack shot with every type of gun. One day, she happened to visit a local fair where a champion *marksman*, named Frank Butler, was showing his skill with guns. Annie *challenged* him to a competition and a shooting match was *arranged*. Annie won easily. She later married Frank Butler, and they set out together across America with their "shooting show". The name of Annie Oakley spread quickly. Chief Sitting Bull nicknamed her 'Little Sure Shot' and was so pleased with her marksmanship that he *adopted* her into his tribe as a daughter. Soon Buffalo Bill was to hear of her great shooting skills and invited her to join his Wild West Show. Thousands of people now flocked to see Annie who was known as "The *Peerless* Lady Wing Shot".

Her shooting power with a rifle or pistol was superb. From a distance of thirty metres, she could hit the thin edge of a card, put a bullet through a penny tossed into the air, or shoot a cigarette held in Frank Butler's lips. She once travelled to Berlin, in Germany, where the Crown Prince William, instead of her husband, held the cigarette. In one of her best tricks, she used a hunting knife as a mirror while she shot and hit a row of targets behind her back! Although she was less than five feet (150 cms) tall, few people would dare stand in the way of this tough woman of the Wild West.

Dictionary work: Find out the meaning of: marksman, challenged, arranged, adopted, peerless. Write each word in a sentence of your own.

Questions

1. Where was Annie Oakley born?
2. Why did she go out to hunt at such an early age?
3. Who was Frank Butler?
4. What nickname did Chief Sitting Bull give her?
5. How did she come to join the Wild West Show?
6. What trick did she perform in Berlin?
7. What was her best trick?
8. Write down a story you know about the Wild West.
9. What have the following got in common: New York, Washington, Chicago, Dallas, Miami? Find them in your atlas.
10. Try to write a sentence for each of these words: outlaw, rodeo, wigwam, ranch, sheriff, cowboy.

Capital Letters

Capital letters are used for:
(i)   The names of places. .... Italy, Spain.
(ii) Words formed from the names of places. Italian, Spanish.
(iii) A person's nationality. .... Spaniard, American.

(A) Insert capital letters where needed in the following sentences.

1. napoleon was a great french general.
2. paris is the capital of france.
3. stephen king speaks fluent spanish and german.
4. the mexican bandit was captured in el paso.
5. barbara's penfriend collects irish stamps.
6. many norwegian fishing trawlers fish off the coasts of canada and greenland.
7. the italian singer sang at the music festival in wexford.
8. frederick chopin, a polish composer, was born near warsaw.
9. in the new supermarket you can buy french wine and dutch cheese.
10. davy crockett died at the alamo.
11. the sligo team will play clare, in ennis on sunday.
12. last february i received a letter from my pen-pal in india.
13. paul watkins bought a swiss watch on friday.
14. the swedish girl arrived in scotland on burn's night.
15. the person rose most admired was mother teresa of calcutta.

(B) Fill in the blank spaces in the following chart. The first one is given.

Country	People	Language
Belgium	Belgian	Flemish, French ....
Canada	....	....
Denmark	....	....
England	....	....
France	....	....
Ireland	....	....
Germany	....	....
Holland	....	....
Poland	....	....
Portugal	....	....
Russia	....	....
Scotland	....	....
Spain	....	....
Sweden	....	....
Switzerland	....	....

The Jumbo Jet

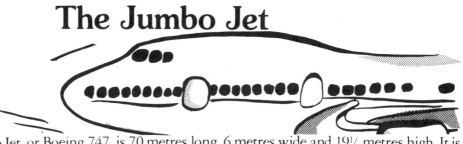

Some facts:

1. The Jumbo Jet, or Boeing 747, is 70 metres long, 6 metres wide and 19½ metres high. It is the largest aircraft ever built for the world's airlines.
2. It seats up to 416 passengers in one flight. In one year, a Jumbo Jet will take 150,000 people between France and America.
3. It carries an amazing 214,000 litres of *fuel* which would be enough to keep a car running for a hundred years. In crossing from New York to London the giant will use 90,000 litres of fuel.
4. It is made up of over four million parts and has over one hundred miles (160 kilometres) of wires and *cables*.
5. Eighteen wheels are needed to get this 300 ton machine into the air.
6. A jumbo jet, flying to New York, will carry over 3,000 kgs of food and drinks to serve to passengers.
7. At a height of 10,600 metres, the Boeing 747 will *cruise* along at a speed of 912 kilometres per hour (560 m.p.h.).

True Story

A Boeing 747 was once on its way from Indonesia to New Zealand with 247 passengers on board. The aircraft met with a thick, deadly cloud of dust and ash thrown into the sky by a volcano. They were flying out over the sea at a height of 10,000 metres when the jet's four engines cut out, one by one. A terrible silence fell on the aircraft. But the quick-thinking pilot put his huge jet into a *glide* and turned back for the airport. For a full thirteen minutes they glided through the air. Even without engines, this great aircraft seemed to take to the skies like a bird. Suddenly, the four engines started again — they had cleared away the ash! Thanks to this *magnificent* machine and its pilot, they were able to safely land half an hour later.

Dictionary work: Find out the meaning of: fuel, cables, cruise, glide, magnificent. Write each word in a sentence of your own.

Questions

1. How heavy is the Jumbo Jet?
2. How much fuel does it carry?
3. How many passengers can it carry?
4. What height and speed does it reach?
5. What did a Jumbo Jet once meet with on its way to New Zealand?
6. Why do you think its engines cut out?
7. What did the pilot do?
8. What have Heathrow, Gatwick, Luton and Stanstead got in common?
9. Who were the Wright Brothers?
10. Write a list of the people who work at an airport.

The Airport

Write a story about a visit to an airport.

Helpful words and ideas.

.... with my best friend .... a tour of .... motorway .... big car park .... a large, modern building .... hundreds of passengers .... hustle and bustle .... tickets .... suitcases .... saying farewell .... visited an aircraft hangar (shed for airplanes) .... vast size .... busy workers .... checking engines .... a huge Jumbo Jet .... allowed on board .... rows of seats .... stairs .... two decks (floors) .... kitchens .... pilot's cockpit .... switches and dials .... lunch .... brought to control tower .... radar screens .... view of runways .... fuel lorries .... roar of airplanes .... taking off .... landing .... took photographs .... a wonderful day.

The Oldest Living Thing In The World

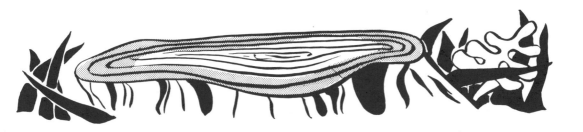

The Giant Sequoia tree of North America was named after "Sikwayi", a Cherokee Indian, who invented a *system* of writing for his tribe. This gigantic tree can grow to a height of 100 metres, which is about as tall as a thirty-*storey* skyscraper. Its trunk is so wide that roads have even been tunnelled through a number of Sequoias without any difficulty. The bark is so thick that it can easily *resist* the attacks of chewing insects. And this thick bark has also helped to protect it from many of the forest fires which so often destroy other trees.

For a long time, scientists were sure that the Giant Sequoia was the oldest living thing in the world — the oldest of which was 3,200 years old. That was until they came upon a tree in Nevada, U.S.A., called the Bristlecone Pine. It was less than 10 metres in height, yet had a massive trunk almost 4 metres wide. These scientists wanted to date the tree by counting its rings, but without damaging it. So, they *drilled* a tiny hole into its side and removed a *sample* of wood from the tree. To their astonishment, they discovered that the Bristlecone Pine was 5,000 years old! This means that it started growing around the time when the Pyramids were being built, and was already 3,000 years old when Jesus was born. Another Bristlecone Pine in California was found to be 4,500 years old. They even found another tree that had over 1,000 rings in a space of only ten centimetres. On looking closely at these rings, it was found that some rings were bigger than others. In other words, the tree grew more in some years than in others. By studying these rings, it was therefore possible to build up a good picture of the weather and growing conditions of past ages.

Dictionary work: Find the meaning of: system; storey; resist; drilled; sample. Write each word in a sentence of your own.

Questions

1. How did the Sequoia tree get its name?
2. How high and wide is the Giant Sequoia?
3. How is the Sequoia able to gain protection from enemy insects?
4. What is the oldest living thing in the world?
5. How is it possible to date a tree?
6. Why are some rings found to be bigger than others?
7. What kind of information can be got from these ancient trees?
8. What are the main uses of trees?
9. List the names of all the trees you know.
10. Can you explain the difference between an evergreen and a deciduous tree?

Over-Used Words

Said

The word 'said' tends to be used too often. Replace it with words from this list: (whispered; complained; shouted; asked; ordered; begged; told; advised).

1. Patrick *said* that the weather was terrible.
2. "Will you give me a loan of your rubber?" *said* Peter.
3. Kate *said* a secret in my ear.
   "Please bring us to the zoo", *said* the children.
5. "The train is coming", *said* Grandad.
6. Mary *said* a story in class yesterday.
7. "Stay in bed for the rest of the week", *said* the doctor.
8. The general *said* that the army was to retreat.

Then

When the word 'then' is used too often, it leads to boring sentences and monotonous stories. Rewrite this story by replacing 'then' with a word from the list. (finally; next; presently; later on; shortly afterwards; almost immediately; soon; at last; soon afterwards; after that; in a little while).

Somewhere in the hills, a tiny spring gushed out of the rock and trickled happily over smooth stones and shiny pebbles. *Then* it was a dancing stream that rushed down the valley, past huge boulders and tall trees of pine. *Then* it was joined by another stream and *then* by another and another. *Then* it became a swift flowing river that roared onwards with great power and force. *Then* it passed a small village at the foot of the hills, where laughing children tossed bits of wood into its racing current. *Then* it flowed under the arch of a sturdy stone bridge where a fisherman sat, his line dangling hopefully into the foaming waters. *Then* it reached the flat, level land of the plain and the river *then* slowed down, becoming silent, dark and deep. *Then* it was winding its way lazily through wide fields of rich green grass. *Then* it came upon a noisy city where huge buildings and tall smokey chimneys crowded the skyline. *Then* it flowed out into the sea.

On Top Of The World

It was only learned in the 1930's that Mount Everest, standing on the border of Tibet and Nepal, was the highest point on earth. The mountain stretches so high up into the *atmosphere* that the air becomes very thin, making it impossible to breathe. So cold is it that neither animal nor plant can survive on its higher slopes. By 1953, at least ten *expeditions* had set out to climb the 8,748 metres (5½ miles) to its *summit*, but all of them failed in the attempt. They met with fierce snowstorms, dangerous ice and bottomless *chasms*. The lives of many brave climbers were lost.

In March of that year, another expedition was mounted to conquer this mighty mountain. Their plan was to set up eight camps along the way to the summit. Then two men would be chosen to make a final climb of 1,000 metres to the top. The climb was as difficult and dangerous as they expected. Slowly but surely they *edged* their way upwards. When the final camp had been set up, two men left to make a last attack on the summit. Hours later, they were forced to return to camp. Like so many others before them, they had been beaten by the giant of Everest. The weather was getting worse and there was time for only one last attempt. Edmund Hillary from New Zealand and Tenzing Norgay of Nepal were picked. With a great effort of bravery, strength and skill, they made their way onwards and upwards. Two days later and they still had not reached the summit. Once more they had to sleep in their tiny tent, only a few hundred metres from the top, as the wind blew and the snow fell all around. There were so near and yet so far! But the 29th May, 1953 was to be their lucky day. To their delight and surprise, Hillary and Tenzing awoke to find calm and sunny weather. Later that morning they became the first people to climb the highest mountain in the world. Since then almost two hundred people have reached the top of Everest.

Dictionary work: Find out the meaning of: atmosphere, expeditions, summit, chasms, edged. Write each word in a sentence of your own.

Questions

1. Where is Mount Everest?
2. How high is it?
3. Give four reasons why Everest is such a difficult mountain to climb.
4. How many expeditions failed to climb the mountain?
5. What was the plan of the next expedition?
6. Who were chosen to make the final attempt on the summit?
7. What were they delighted to see on the morning of May 29th 1953?
8. List the qualities needed to make a good mountain climber.
9. Write a paragraph about an exciting sport you would like to try.
10. Try to find out the name, height and location of Britain's tallest mountain.

Singular and Plural

Singular means only one
Plural means more than one

Examples:
We say one cat but two cats
We say one box but two boxes

(A) Add -s or -es to the words in italics to mean more than one.

1. The *boy* put the *cake* in the *oven.*
2. The *farmer* lifted the *rock* from the *field.*
3. The *cook* prepared the *dish* in the kitchen.
4. The *bishop* visited the *church* in the *town.*
5. His *uncle* gave him the *watch.*
6. The *soldier* loaded the *gun* with the *bullet.*
7. The *bird* flew from the *bush.*
8. The *plumber* fixed the *pipe* in the *cottage.*
9. The *pirate* attacked the *ship* near the *island.*
10. The *class* found the *shell* on the *beach.*

Words ending in -ay, -ey, -oy, -uy, get their plural by adding -s.

(B) Write the plural of the underlined words.

1. He ate the *biscuit* on the *tray.*
2. The *train* sped through the *valley.*
3. She left the *key* in the *pocket.*
4. He bought the *tie* and the *jersey.*
5. The *ray* of light came through the *window.*
6. Snow covered the *roof* and *chimney.*
7. The *boat* sailed away from the *quay.*
8. The *horse* and *jockey* cleared the *fence.*
9. The *cow* and the *donkey* ate the *vegetable.*
10. They served the *turkey* at the *dinner.*

(C) Write the following sentences in the singular

1. The ladies read the books on the trains.
2. The dentists extracted the children's teeth.
3. The enemies lived in far away countries.
4. The foxes ate the salmon.
5. The fish were swimming in the deep pools.
6. The potatoes were served with fish.
7. The shops sell pliers and shears.
8. The farmers put the turkeys in the sheds.
9. The brushes were left on the roofs.
10. The husbands and wives played with the babies.

Silver Streak

The life story of a salmon begins in the sandy gravel bed of a mountain stream. There, in the sand the female salmon digs a tiny nest with her tail. It is called a "**redd**". In this shallow nest she lays *batches* of pink eggs. Within a week she may lay as many as 15,000 of them, each egg the size of a pellet. Her husband fertilises them. The mother salmon then covers the eggs with fine grains of sand. Their work completed, the parents begin the return journey to the sea. Tired and in need of food, many of them die on the way to the sea.

It takes 2-3 months for the eggs to hatch. The young fish are called "**alevins**". They feed on a yolk sac attached to their body. When the yolk is eaten they feed on tiny water insects and fleas. Many of them are devoured by hungry eels and herons. They grow slowly and their pale brown bodies *develop* stripes. At this stage of their life the young fish are given the name "**parr**". Every day they have great fun chasing each other up and down the clear pools of the stream.

After a few months a strange event takes place. The eager parrs become tired of life in the freshwater. Thousands and thousands of them head downstream to the sea. The young fish are now called "**smolts**". It is a beautiful sight to watch them floating downriver, tails first. These fish float tail-first because if they went the other way they would drown — the water would get into their gills. They glide and *slither* over rocks and boulders.

On reaching the mouth of the river they twirl around before setting off to explore the deep ocean. No one is certain how far out to sea they swim. Indeed scientists are still trying to discover the whereabouts of their new homes. While at sea they grow fat on a rich diet of shrimps and prawns. Alas! many of them are eaten by hungry seals and turtles. Those that survive grow fat and strong and develop into beautiful silvery fish just like their parents. They remain 5-6 years in the sea waters before returning home to spawn in their mountain streams. The return journey is known as the "**salmon run**". Before setting out for home the wise salmon store up enough food in their bodies to last them the long trip. It is one of the marvels of nature how young salmon make their way back to their place of birth. Experts think they do this by their keen sense of smell.

The silvery salmon leap and flash over great waterfalls and *weirs* as they fight their way up river. Hundreds of them are bashed and dashed against sharp rocks and jagged *boulders*. Some salmon travel as much as 20 kilometres in a single day. Others make little progress against the swift currents and seem to be shoved backwards.

Day after day they swim nearer to their mountain homes. As they turn off into the different streams they choose a partner. At last, tired and weary, husband and wife reach their *destination*. Once again the amazing life story of the salmon begins.

Dictionary work: Find out the meaning of: batches, develop, slither, weirs, boulders, destination. Write each word in a sentence of your own.

Questions

1. What is a redd?
2. When is the young salmon called a parr?
3. Why does the smolt float down with its tail first?
4. What does the salmon feed on at sea?
5. What is the 'salmon run'?
6. How far can a salmon travel in a day?

Nouns

The word 'noun' means name. A noun is the name of any person, place or thing. Here are four 'naming' words: John, frog, desert, brush. 'John' is the name of a person. 'Frog' is the name of an animal. 'Desert' is the name of a place. 'Brush' is the name of a thing. John, frog, desert and brush are nouns.

(A) Pick out the nouns in the following sentences.

1. The horse galloped down the field.
2. Mary hurt her elbow when she fell off her bike.
3. The panda was caught in a forest in China.
4. The waiter put the coffee, milk and sugar on the table.
5. The soldiers charged when the corporal blew the bugle.
6. The match was played before a large crowd at Croke Park.
7. The hawk had a nest with two eggs at the top of the cliff.
8. He spotted a bright diamond flashing in the rock.
9. Huge waves crashed against the rocks below the lighthouse.
10. Jesus was born in a stable at Bethlehem.

(B) Write a list of nouns under each heading.

Clothes	Sports	Countries	Animals
....	....	....	....
....	....	....	....
....	....	....	....
....	....	....	....

(C) Give the correct noun (or name) for each of the following.

1. A person who gives lessons. ....
2. The place where an Eskimo lives. ....
3. The animal which tempted Adam and Eve. ....
4. A person who fights fires. ....
5. The place where a clown performs. ....
6. The animal known as the 'king of the jungle'. ....
7. A thing which is used for measuring time. ....
8. A person who travels in space. ....
9. An animal with a very long neck. ....
10. A place where paintings are put on display. ....

Short Stories

1. Write a short story:

Helpful words and ideas.

.... damp, misty day .... walking .... huge, powerful lorry .... roared past .... sharp bend .... screech of brakes .... skidded .... spun across .... deafening (loud) crash .... overturned .... goods scattered .... dashed .... dialled 999 .... police and ambulance .... hospital.

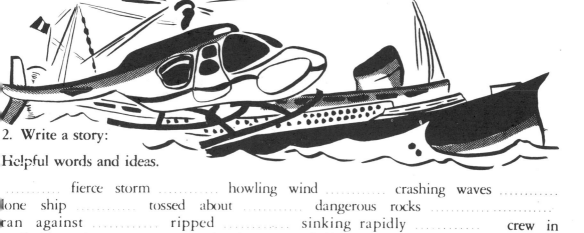

2. Write a story:

Helpful words and ideas.

.... fierce storm .... howling wind .... crashing waves .... lone ship .... tossed about .... dangerous rocks .... ran against .... ripped .... sinking rapidly .... crew in peril (danger) .... s.o.s. signal............ helicopter .... hovered .... rescue operation .... hoisted (lifted) to safety .... wreckage ....

The Raiders From The North

Around the year 850 A.D. Viking raiders sailed around the coast and up the main rivers of Ireland. They plundered monasteries and villages, spreading terror wherever they went. In the following story, a young Irish girl, who lived beside the River Shannon tells how she first saw these savage warriors.

I will always remember the day I first saw those wolves of the sea. It was a fine summer's morning and the people of the village were already up and about their daily duties. My father had gone with some of the men to bring the cows out to *pasture*. My mother had left at sunrise to bring some cheeses and honey to the monks of the monastery across the woodland. It was her *custom* to do this each week. But lately she had been returning with dark news which she would whisper to my father. I had guessed what was wrong, for it was no secret in the village. Raiders from the North had swept like a red wave on to the shores of Ireland. They came with the sword and the flame. They left death and *destruction* behind.

I was sitting with my grandfather outside our hut, when Niall, my little brother, came running up to me.

"Will you bring me to the otters now, Niamh?", he asked hopefully. A pair of otters had built their home on the great river which flowed through the woods. The otters were our secret and we visited them each day. Although the sun had hardly risen above the tree-tops, I agreed to go. We made our way across the fields and took the path into the sunlit woods. Blue flowers of early summer were everywhere and I had a fine bunch of them picked by the time we came to the river. We tiptoed up to our hiding spot, for otters are shy, gentle creatures and are easily frightened. Our hideout was in some long grass overlooking a quiet pool in the river where they would play. It was not long before our two furry friends appeared. We sat down and looked on happily as they swam and dived, tumbled and turned, wriggled and rolled about in the water. All of a sudden, they disappeared. There was a strange silence on the river. Then I heard the steady *rhythm* of the oars cutting the water. Looking up, I saw the three longboats come into view as a shiver of fear ran down my back. The top of each ship was in the shape of a dragon's head and the end was carved into a tail. The side of the first ship was painted black and yellow, the second was purple and gold, the third was red and white. All three were packed with raiders — the raiders from the North. Some were armed with arrow and bow, some held sword and shield, while others stood *clutching* the great battleaxe of war. My heart nearly stopped when my little brother, not knowing who they were, stood up to watch. I did not wait to see what would happen next. I pulled Niall away and we ran for our lives.

Racing through the woods, dashing across the meadow, we arrived breathless at the gates of our village. My mother, who had returned from the monastery, lifted my crying brother in her arms. Worried villagers gathered around me as I tried to tell them what I had seen. Panic now spread like wildfire. People took with them whatever they could and made their escape across the marshlands and towards the hills. My father leaped on his horse and galloped away to warn the holy men of the monastery. It was not long before I heard the bells of alarm ringing out in the morning air.

Dictionary work: Find out the meaning of: pasture, custom, destruction, rhythm, clutching. Write each word in a sentence of your own.

Questions

1. Who were the "wolves of the sea"?
2. Where was the childrens' mother on that morning?
3. Where did Niall want to go?
4. Why did the children go on their tiptoes to the hiding spot?
5. Describe one of the boats they saw.
6. How were the raiders armed?
7. Write down what you think Niamh said when she ran into the village.
8. Why did her father gallop away on his horse?
9. Why do you think the villagers did not stay and fight the raiders?
10. Think up an ending for the story and write it in your own words.

Nouns

A noun is the name of a person, place, animal or thing. It is a 'naming' word.

Here is a list of naming words.

1. boy
2. sandcastle
3. donkey
4. seagull
5. sand
6. cliff
7. sailing boat
8. sky
9. girl
10. rock
11. hat
12. ship
13. saddle
14. flag
15. shell
16. sea
17. swimmer
18. pool
19. child
20. water
21. strand
22. beach
23. sail
24. pebble.

Pick out the nouns in the following sentences.

1. Rabbits dig burrows in the ground.
2. My dog lives in a kennel.
3. The bullfrog leaped into the pond.
4. There are many giraffes and lions in Africa.
5. The eagle has a nest in the mountains.
6. Honeybees make honey in hives.
7. John Smith bought a donkey and a goat.
8. The sheepdog buried a bone in the garden.
9. The spider spun a web in the garage.
10. The wasp stung Mary on the nose.

Fill in the blank spaces with suitable nouns.

1. A cat has four .... and two ....
2. Cows eat .... and ....
3. A young dog is called a ....
4. The swan swam gracefully in the ....
5. The goat butted the .... with its horns.
6. The ant carried .... to the ....
7. The .... is the tallest animal in the world.
8. The hunter shot a wild .... in the ....
9. The wolf and the .... live in the ....
10. An elephant's long nose is called a ....

28

Addressing an Envelope

This is how the name and address should be written.

> Mr. Brian McKenna,
> 64 Greenwood Rd.,
> Whalley,
> Lancashire BB9 4PF

The name is written on the first line.
The street, road or townland is written on the second line.
The name of the town is placed on the third line.
The county and postcode is placed on the fourth line.

Note:

(i) The first line of the address should start well away from the top of the envelope and a little to the right.

(ii) Have each line in the address a little farther to the right than the previous one.

(iii) A comma is placed at the end of each line, except the last line where a full stop must be used.

Abbreviations: It is often useful to shorten the names of people and places. A full stop must be placed after abbreviated words.

Names: Instead of 'Mister' write Mr.. When writing to a woman use Mrs., Miss, or Ms. before the name.

Places: These are the most common abbreviations.

Road	Rd.	County	Co.
Street	St.	Drive	Dr.
Avenue	Ave.	Boulevard	Blvd.
Square	Sq.	Terrace	Tce.
Park	Pk.	Gardens	Gdns.
Grove	Gro.	Crescent	Cres.

(A) Write your own name and address on this envelope.

(B) Draw envelopes and address them, using abbreviations where necessary.

1. Bernard Farrell, 36 Antrim Drive, Otley, Yorkshire. LS21 1DX
2. Mrs. Joan McGrath, 48 Connolly Leek, Staffordshire. ST10 2LX
3. Joseph Byrne, 107 Seaview Gardens, Southend, Essex. SS10 1BY
4. Pauline Baker, 17 Market Street, St. Just, Cornwall. TR19 7SJ
5. Patrick Burke, 6 Glendale Park, Cheddar, Sommerset. BS27 4BL
6. Anne Byrne, 18 Greenfield Road, Southend, Argyll. PA28 7PJ

The Eel

The eel begins its life in the Sargasso Sea. This sea, with its vast jungle of floating seaweed, is the breeding ground for European and American eels.

The female eel may lay as many as fifteen million eggs. These are *fertilised* by the male eel. Having completed their *mission* in life, both parents die. Soon afterwards, the eggs hatch out into tiny flat larvae. *Gradually* these grow and develop into worm-like creatures about 3 cms. long. These curious baby eels are tossed about in the ocean currents and drift northwards. A strange and mysterious migration takes place. Millions of wriggling baby eels swim in the direction of their *ancestral* homes. The European eels journey eastward to reach Europe and North Africa. Their friends, the American eels, travel westward to the American mainland. It is one of the marvels of nature that these two *species* of eels never travel in the wrong direction.

It takes the European eel about three years to reach the coasts and mainlands of Europe. By then the baby eels, called elvers, are about seven cms. long and have developed all the fins, gills and scales of an adult eel.

On reaching the European mainland the female eel swims inland and makes her way slowly up our rivers, streams, lakes and ponds. Meanwhile, the male eel awaits her return near the mouth of the rivers and seashores. The journey up-river for the female eel can be long and tiresome, covering a few hundred kilometres. She wriggles, glides and crawls over dams, waterfalls, marshy lands and through sewerage pipes to reach her destination.

Just like the frog, she breathes mainly through the tiny blood vessels in her damp skin. She remains many years in her new inland home, feeding on water insects, snails, smaller fish and *garbage*. At night she wriggles out from under muddy stones and rock crevices in search of food. She has to keep a sharp look out for her enemies, the hungry otter and greedy heron.

Having remained for 7-15 years in our rivers and lakes the female eels get a strange *longing* to return to their breeding grounds in the Sargasso Sea. They make the long journey downriver till they reach the ocean. There, they are greeted by the *patient* male eels. Together they swim thousands of kilometres across the Atlantic Ocean. On returning home mother eel and father eel mate, leave their eggs to be hatched and quietly die. Their children will follow the same amazing migratory journey that their parents travelled. Once again this life cycle of the eel begins.

Dictionary work: Find out the meaning of: fertilised; mission; gradually; ancestral; species; garbage; longing; patient. Write each word in a sentence of your own.

Questions

1. Where do eels breed?
2. What is a young eel called?
3. How do eels breathe?
4. Where do they spend most of their lives?
5. How does the female eel make her way inland?
6. Name some of the eel's enemies.
7. What do eels feed on?
8. How many years does the female eel remain inland?

The electric eel

The powerful electric eel is found in South American waters. Its mighty electrical discharge of 500 volts is strong enough to stun you. No wonder this vicious creature has few enemies.

The eel's body contains a great electrical battery. This spectacular battery helps to locate and kill its victim. The current it generates flows through the eel. Naturally the eel has no desire to electrocute itself, so its essential body organs are insulated by layers of fatty tissue.

Sounds and Movements

Study page 93 if you are unable to do any of the following exercises.

(A) Fill in the blank spaces.

1. The eagle screams and swoops.
2. The owl ..... and .....
3. The robin ..... and .....
4. The crow ..... and .....
5. The pigeon ..... and .....
6. The duck ..... and .....
7. The lark ..... and .....
8. The hen ..... and .....
9. The sparrow ..... and .....
10. The seagull ..... and .....

(B) Fill in the blank spaces.

1. The horse neighs and gallops.
2. The dog ..... and .....
3. The wolf ..... and .....
4. The bull ..... and .....
5. The pig ..... and .....
6. The lion ..... and .....
7. The monkey ..... and .....
8. The lamb ..... and .....
9. The bear ..... and .....
10. The mouse ..... and .....

(C) Fill in the blank spaces.

1. The beat of a drum
2. The ..... of a train
3. The ..... of a horn
4. The ..... of a clock
5. The ..... of brakes
6. The ..... of wings
7. The ..... of a whip
8. The ..... of coins
9. The ..... of water
10. The rush of .....
11. The swish of .....
12. The wail of a .....
13. The sizzling of .....
14. The pitter patter of .....
15. The ping of a .....
16. The popping of .....

Writing a Letter

Letters can be either long or short. For example we would expect a long letter from a close friend, or from a member of the family who has gone abroad. Letters of invitation, thanks, apology, on the other hand tend to be short. But the layout of all letters is the same.

Read carefully the following letter.

> 19 High Street,
> Brighton.
> Sussex. BR2 2AB
> 9/7/88
>
> Dear Mary,
>
> I would like you to come to my birthday party next Saturday. The party will start around 5 o'clock.
> I do hope that your cold is better and that you will be able to come.
>
> Your good friend,
> Angela.

1. The writer's full **address** is written at the top right-hand side of the page. Each line of the address is a little to the right of the previous line, as shown.

2. The **date** is written under the last line of the address. The date given above could also have been written in the following ways: 9/7/1987 or 9 July 1987.

3. The **greeting** is placed on the left-hand side. Note the use of capital letters and the placing of the comma at the end of the greeting.

4. The **message** begins on the line below the greeting.

5. The **ending** is written on the right-hand side and the writer's name is placed below it. Note the use of capital letters, comma and full stop.

Examples:
Your fond son,   Yours sincerely,
Best wishes,   Yours faithfully,
Yours,   Yours truly,

Exercises

1. Write a reply to Angela's letter. Your letter should (a) thank Angela for her letter. (b) Accept her invitation. (c) Tell her that you are looking forward to the party.
2. Write a long letter to your pen-pal in Spain.
3. Write a letter to a radio station asking for a record to be played 'on the air' for your brother's birthday.
4. Write out correctly the following letter,

28 Harbour Rd, Grimsby, Lincolnshire. Gr3 1BC. 6th July 1988. Dear Uncle Dan, it was was very kind of you to send me the money for my birthday. Your gift was most welcome as I have been saving for a bike since Easter. I look forward to meeting you at Sue's wedding in Skegness next month. Yours sincerely, Vincent

The Hedgehog
Comprehension

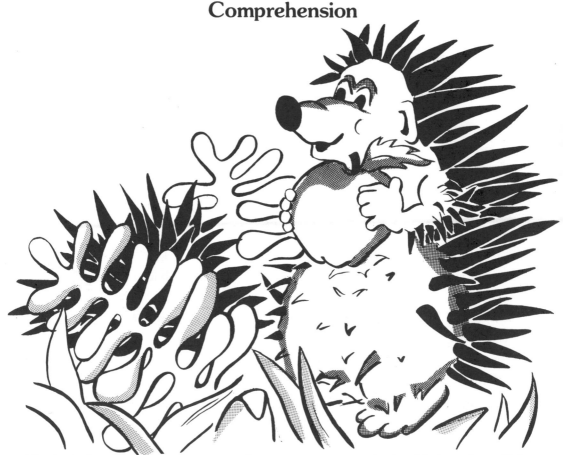

The hedgehog lives in a cosy nest under a tree stump or a hedge. He has a beautiful coat of spines. These prickly spines protect him from his enemies, the fox and the badger. His sharp hearing and *keen* sense of smell warn him of approaching danger. When *threatened*, he curls into a tight ball, tucks his head and paws beneath the soft underside of his stomach, *extends* his spines and remains motionless. His enemies usually *retire* with bleeding noses. How would you like to be tickled by one of the hedgehog's 16,000 dagger-like spines?

These spines also act as a cushion for him if he falls or rolls down a steep slope. He can even carry fruit with his spines. When he has gathered a pile of crab-apples he rolls over them. In this way the fruit sticks to the spines and is carried back to the nest.

Thousands of fleas and ticks, called *parasites*, live among the spines of the hedgehog. The unfortunate creature cannot *groom* or preen his coat of spines, so he is a happy nesting ground for ticks and fleas.

The hedgehog's diet is a varied one. His powerful jaws and needle-sharp teeth crush and grind both plant and animal food. On a wet night you can hear him grunting and snorting as he moves about in search of food. His long snout helps him discover hidden snails, beetles and woodlice under the dead leaves and the brushwood. He uses his sharp front claws when digging for slugs and grubs. He is the gardener's friend because he helps him to get rid of pests that ruin the garden.

The hedgehog is able to eat bees, wasps and poisonous snakes without any danger of harming himself. He may be riddled with stings in the face, suffer a puffed and swollen snout but he does not die. Few creatures can attack and kill the poisonous viper snake. This deadly reptile can kill a guinea-pig within seconds. However, it is no match for the hedgehog. He spikes the snake's head and fangs and bites it on the back of the neck until it dies.

The hedgehog has a *curious* habit of licking objects with the tip of his tongue. This action creates a frothy lather in the animal's mouth. He twists and turns as he tries to smear the foam over his spines. This amazing behaviour is called "self-annointing". Nobody knows why he bathes himself with his own saliva.

During the year the female hedgehog has two broods. The first one is born in early summer and the second one in the autumn. There are usually 4-6 young in a brood. At birth the baby hedgehogs are blind and deaf and have only a few rubbery spines. The mother lovingly protects her babies as they are helpless and cannot curl into a ball. Like all mammals, she suckles her young until they are strong and healthy. After a few weeks the little hedgehogs develop layers of muscles strong enough to raise the prickly spines. At night they are taken from the nest by the mother and shown where to look for food. The family of hedgehogs scurries along in single file, the mother leading the *procession*. When the babies are strong enough they seek their own fortunes in the hedgerows and ditches.

In winter the hedgehog hibernates. He goes for a deep sleep in an old rabbit burrow or under a thick hedge. His cosy nest is lined with layers of dead leaves and straw. During the cold and frosty weather he sleeps soundly under a thick blanket of leaves. On warm sunny days he will awaken and shuffle about in the undergrowth. When he re-appears in spring he is very weak and must find food without delay or he will die.

Hedgehogs live until they are about 40 years old. Scientists tell us that they have been living on this earth for about twenty five million years.

Dictionary work: Find out the meaning of: keen; threatened; extend; retire; parasite; groom; curious; procession. Write each word in a sentence of your own.

Questions

1. How do you think the hedgehog got his name?
2. How does he defend himself?
3. What enemies has he?
4. Where would you expect to find hedgehogs?
5. How are the spines useful to the hedgehog?
6. What is the hedgehog's favourite food?
7. What does he hunt by night?
8. When are young hedgehogs born?
9. Why are baby hedgehogs defenceless?
10. How does a hedgehog kill a viper?

Exercises

(A) Write the following list of words in alphabetical order.

1. hedgehog, hyena, horse, hare, hippopotamus.
2. buffalo, badger, beaver, bat, bear.
3. mule, monkey, moose, mole, mouse.
4. stoat, sheep, squirrel, skunk, seal.
5. gorilla, giraffe, goat, gazelle.

(B) The hedgehog has a covering of spines. Which creatures have a covering of:

(i) scales   (ii) wool   (iii) feathers   (iv) fur   (v) hair.

(C) Hedgehogs can be kept as pets.
Remember to sprinkle your hedgehog frequently with flea powder, as he may be infested with parasites. Hedgehogs eat a wide variety of food. They particularly like a bowl of milk and bread. Each week clean out the hedgehog's hutch.

(D) Draw a colourful picture of a hedgehog.
Write 10 interesting sentences about your picture. Remember to describe his:
short stumpy legs, prickly spines, tiny ears, sharp teeth, snout, greedy appetite and strange habits.

(E) Name 5 creatures that hibernate in winter.

(i) . . . .   (ii) . . . .   (iii) . . . .   (iv) . . . .   (v) . . . .

Nature Trail

The Frog

(A) Underline the correct word in brackets.

1. A frog *(roars, barks, croaks)*.
2. A frog eats *(nuts, lettuce, insects)*.
3. A frog has webbed *(ears, eyes, feet)*.
4. A frog is smaller than an *(ladybird, flea, alligator)*.
5. A frog is an *(animal, insect, amphibian)*.
6. A baby frog is called a *(toad, newt, tadpole)*.
7. A grown frog has *(lungs, fins, gills)*.
8. A frog cannot *(fly, leap, swim)*.
9. A grown frog has no *(tail, nose, ears)*.
10. A frog's eggs are called *(pupae, larvae, spawn)*.

(B) From the given clues fill in the missing letters.

1. A girl's dress.   Fr ....
2. Apples, pears and bananas.   Fr ....
3. Once a tadpole.   Fr ....
4. A French coin.   Fr ....
5. The opposite of "stale".   Fr ....
6. A week day.   Fr ....
7. A girl's name.   Fr ....
8. A brown spot on your face.   Fr ....
9. The opposite of "back".   Fr ....
10. Paris is the capital of this country. Fr ....

Fr.

The Red Apples
Creative Writing

Helpful words and ideas:

.... strolling home with friend .... quiet laneway .... orchard ....
...... trees bulging with fruit .... could not resist temptation .... nobody in the vicinity
.... orchard wall .... crept on tiptoes .... climbed apple tree ....
.... ripe red apples .... hurriedly picked .... munching gleefully ....
.... a sudden shocking surprise .... ferocious barking .... loud, angry shouts
.... man waving stick .... startled and terrified .... dropped fruit ....
.... dashed across .... scrambled over .... dog snapping at our
feet .... hearts thumping .... fled in terror .... scurried homewards ....
remained inside .... never again.

William Tell
Comprehension

Many many years ago Switzerland was conquered by an Austrian army. The Austrian governor of the little village of Altdorf was a wicked man named Gessler. In the village square he ordered a flag pole to be erected. The proud Gessler placed his feather hat on top of the pole. He wished to *humiliate* the Swiss people, by ordering them to kneel and bow before his hat.

William Tell, the best archer in Switzerland, happened to pass by the flag pole. He refused to bow to the governor's hat. As he was leaving the village with his son, the angry Gessler shouted, "Arrest that man."

Immediately the Austrian soldiers arrested William Tell. "People tell me you are a great marksman," jeered Gessler. "Let's see how good you are."

The cruel tyrant made William's young son, Jimmy, stand against an oak tree. On his head he placed an apple.

"You must split the apple in two, if you hope to go free," commanded Gessler.

Tell placed an arrow in his bow and took careful aim. The silent crowd watched anxiously. Suddenly the arrow whistled through the air. The apple split in two and the arrow buried itself in the tree. A great shout *rent* the air. The people cheered with joy. William Tell's courage and skill had foiled the governor's cruel plan.

"I see you are carrying a second arrow," snarled Gessler.

"Yes," replied William, "and if my son had been injured, I *intended* this second arrow for your black heart."

On hearing this, the Austrian ruler went wild with anger. "Soldiers, bind this man and take him across the lake to the castle *dungeons*."

William Tell was bound and thrown into a boat which was to carry him across the lake to the castle prison. His friends took his young son and hid him in a safe place.

While crossing the lake a terrible storm arose. William was an expert sailor and the soldiers unbound him and asked him to take the helm. In the twinkling of an eye, the clever oarsman steered the boat near a rocky ledge, sprang ashore and escaped into the mountains.

According to legend, when Gessler and his soldiers were searching the mountains for the prisoner, William saw the wicked governor, placed an arrow in his bow, took aim and fired. This time the arrow pierced the heart of Gessler, the tyrant. He fell from his horse, *mortally* wounded. At last the people of Altdorf had a new ruler and a hero — William Tell.

Dictionary work: Find out the meaning of: humiliate; immediately; rent; foiled; intended; dungeon; mortal. Write each word in a sentence of your own.

Questions

1. Where did the events in the story take place?
2. Who was Gessler?
3. How did he try to humiliate the Swiss people?
4. What was the name of William Tell's son?
5. How did Tell display his skill in archery?
6. What was the reason for the second arrow?
7. How did the tyrant Gessler die?
8. How do you know that Tell was an expert sailor?
9. Why do you think, did the people of Altdorf choose Tell as their leader?
10. The story you have just read is a legend. Write a sentence to explain each of the following words: (i) fairy-tale (ii) myth.
11. William Tell was a famous Swiss archer.
    Write an interesting sentence about each of the following people.
    (i) Robin Hood   (ii) Peter Pan   (iii) Huckleberry Finn
    (iv) Cinderella   (v) Goldilocks   (vi) Rip Van Winkle

Complete the following expressions.
Example: bow and arrow.

1. needle and ....
2. hammer and ....
3. scissors and ....
4. spade and ....
5. lock and ....
6. knife and ....
7. pen and ....
8. hook and ....
9. pepper and ....
10. iron and ....
11. soap and ....
12. sea and ....

Confusing Words

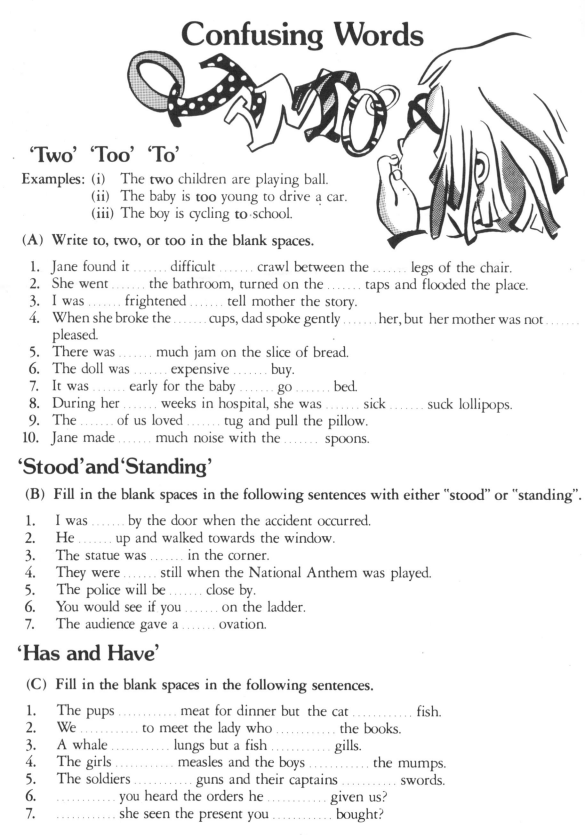

'Two' 'Too' 'To'

Examples: (i)   The **two** children are playing ball.
 (ii)   The baby is **too** young to drive a car.
 (iii) The boy is cycling **to** school.

(A) Write to, two, or too in the blank spaces.

1. Jane found it .... difficult .... crawl between the .... legs of the chair.
2. She went .... the bathroom, turned on the .... taps and flooded the place.
3. I was .... frightened .... tell mother the story.
4. When she broke the .... cups, dad spoke gently .... her, but her mother was not ....
    pleased.
5. There was .... much jam on the slice of bread.
6. The doll was .... expensive .... buy.
7. It was .... early for the baby .... go .... bed.
8. During her .... weeks in hospital, she was .... sick .... suck lollipops.
9. The .... of us loved .... tug and pull the pillow.
10. Jane made .... much noise with the .... spoons.

'Stood' and 'Standing'

(B) Fill in the blank spaces in the following sentences with either "stood" or "standing".

1. I was .... by the door when the accident occurred.
2. He .... up and walked towards the window.
3. The statue was .... in the corner.
4. They were .... still when the National Anthem was played.
5. The police will be .... close by.
6. You would see if you .... on the ladder.
7. The audience gave a .... ovation.

'Has and Have'

(C) Fill in the blank spaces in the following sentences.

1. The pups .... meat for dinner but the cat .... fish.
2. We .... to meet the lady who .... the books.
3. A whale .... lungs but a fish .... gills.
4. The girls .... measles and the boys .... the mumps.
5. The soldiers .... guns and their captains .... swords.
6. .... you heard the orders he .... given us?
7. .... she seen the present you .... bought?

Unusual Birds
Comprehension

The Humming Bird

The tiny humming bird gets its name from the sound it makes when flapping its wings. This colourful bird flaps its wings 50-60 times a second. How quickly can you click or snap your fingers in a second? Perhaps twice! By rapidly beating its wings, the humming bird can remain in the same position, fly backwards and even rise straight up like a helicopter.

It feeds on the nectar of flowers and little insects while *hovering* in flight. Its long thin beak and hairy tongue are especially suited to *prod* and *probe* the hearts of flowers. This bird is remarkable for its *array* of red, blue and green colours. Although it is the smallest bird in the world, it will fearlessly attack crows and hawks that invade its territory and nest.

The cuplike nest it builds is an architectural wonder. A *mass* of grasses, mosses and *fibres* are woven together with strands of cobwebs, to form a tiny nest about the size of a walnut shell. The nest holds two snow-white eggs. These are the smallest birds' eggs in the world. When the eggs are hatched, the mother feeds the nestlings by thrusting her bill down their throats. Then, *vibrating* her body, she regurgitates (throws up) the sweet nectar from her stomach.

The pretty humming bird is found in the tropical regions of North and South America and in Cuba.

The Arctic Tern

The Arctic Tern is often called the "sea-swallow", because it has a forked tail and swoops and glides like a swallow.

The tern is the champion long-distance traveller. It builds its nest and breeds in the northern regions of Europe, Asia and North America. When it has reared its young, this amazing bird flies south to enjoy summer in the Antarctic, a distance of about 18,000 kilometres. It takes about three months to complete this astonishing journey.

The following year the return trip is made by the world's greatest globe-trotter — The Arctic Tern.

Dictionary work: Find out the meaning of: hover; prod; probe; array; mass; fibre; vibrate. Write each word in a sentence of your own.

Questions

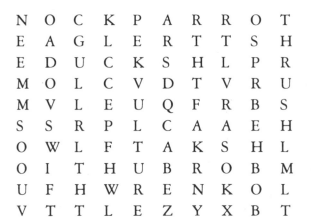

1. Where would you find the humming bird?
2. Why does it beat its wings so rapidly?
3. How does it build its nest?
4. How does the mother feed her young?
5. What record does the Arctic Tern hold?
6. What record does the humming bird hold?

Wordsearch

Can you find the names of twelve birds in this grid?

```
N  O  C  K  P  A  R  R  O  T
E  A  G  L  E  R  T  T  S  H
E  D  U  C  K  S  H  L  P  R
M  O  L  C  V  D  T  V  R  U
M  V  L  E  U  Q  F  R  B  S
S  S  R  P  L  C  A  A  E  H
O  W  L  F  T  A  K  S  H  L
O  I  T  H  U  B  R  O  B  M
U  F  H  W  R  E  N  K  O  L
V  T  T  L  E  Z  Y  X  B  T
```

Irish Birds

Tick off any of these birds you have seen.

Barn owl	Hooded crow	Oystercatcher
Blackbird	Kingfisher	Pheasant
Blue tit	Kittiwake	Shelduck
Bullfinch	Lapwing	Skylark
Chaffinch	Linnet	Songthrush
Coal tit	Long-eared owl	Starling
Coot	Magpie	Swan
Dabchick	Mallard	Wood pigeon
Fulmar	Meadow pipit	Wren
Greenfinch	Mistle thrush	Snipe
Hedgesparrow	Moorhen	Yellowhammer

Adjectives

Words which name things are called nouns, **for example**; car, dog, house, cake, soldier, rocket. In speaking and writing we may wish to describe these nouns, to give a better picture of them. Thus we might say: a **bright, new** car; a **shaggy, old** dog; a **little, one-storey** house; the **delicious** cake; the **brave** soldier, a **powerful** rocket. These words which describe the nouns are called adjectives.

A) Underline the adjectives in these sentences.

1. Their tired eyes looked out across the vast desert.
2. Our simple but clever plan was to hide in the wooden barn.
3. The ugly witch rode across the dark sky on a magical broomstick.
4. They tied a long string to a red rosy apple.
5. On Hallowe'en we dressed up as ugly goblins and dangerous demons.
6. The hungry thrush fed on a fat, juicy worm.
7. The little girl's pet rabbit loved its cosy new home.
8. The first train was fast and comfortable.
9. The thin ice cracked under the weight of the heavy skater.
10. The silver salmon slept in the deep, dark pool.

B) Underline the adjectives in the following paragraph.

The Aitkin family rose early on the first morning of their holiday in Wales. The weather was warm and sunny — a perfect day for a nice picnic at the seaside. The happy and excited children helped their parents prepare a big feast of tasty sandwiches and home-made cakes. After a quick breakfast they set off on foot for a small sandy beach about a mile from their thatched cottage. Already, the clear, blue sky was filled with the sweet, joyful song of tiny larks. As they strolled down the dusty road, their eager eyes gazed upon the broad, calm ocean.

C) Choose the correct adjective from the following list to fill the blank spaces in the story.
(touching; generous; small; kind; big; soft; old; cold; feathery; shivering; outstretched).

He was an .... man and he lived in the .... house next to ours. He was very ......
.... to the birds during the .... months of winter. Each morning he used to bring them
.... morsels of .... bread. The .... birds used to perch on his
.... arm and eat the crumbs of bread. It was a very .... sight to
see this .... man with his .... friends around him.

Extending Sentences

Short simple sentences can be made more interesting by adding suitable words and phrases. One of the best ways of doing this is by answering one of the questions: **When? Where? How? Why?**

Examples: (i)   The trees shed their leaves. When?
               The trees shed their leaves **in autumn**.
      (ii)   The squirrel built a drey. Where?
               The squirrel built a drey **high up in a tree**.
      (iii)   The lark was singing. How?
               The lark was singing **sweetly**.
      (iv)   The fox crossed the stream. Why?
               The fox crossed the stream **to escape from the hounds**.

(A) Extend the following sentences by answering the questions.

1. The otter has a home .... Where?
2. The huntsmen arrived .... When?
3. The rabbit is frightened .... Why?
4. The spider trapped the fly .... How?
5. The cuckoo lays her eggs .... Where?
6. Swallows come to England .... When?
7. The snail crawled under the leaf .... Why?
8. The monkey amused the children .... How?

Joining Sentences

We often use the word "**and**" or "**but**" to join two sentences.

Examples: (i)   **She came into the room. She switched on the light.**
               She came into the room and switched on the light.
      (ii)   Harry is working. Mary is sleeping.
               Harry is working **but** Mary is sleeping.

(B) Join the two sentences together by using either 'and' or 'but'

1. The bull chased him. Luckily he escaped.
2. The policeman blew his whistle. The man stopped.
3. It is raining today. It was fine yesterday.
4. Our cat has a tail. A Manx cat has no tail.
5. The player scored a goal. The crowd cheered.
6. I knocked loudly on the door. She did not open it.
7. A large fire burned in the grate. The room was warm.
8. The cow was milked. The calves were fed.

Two Essays

The Clowns

Helpful words.

comically dressed .... cherry-red noses .... powdered faces ....
rosy red cheeks .... puffed and swollen .... vivid scarlet shirt ......
..... baggy trousers .... enormous boots .... funny headgear ...
.... danced .... skipped .... jumped .... leaped,
rolled and romped .... funny antics .... peals of laughter ......
...... walked clumsily .... clip! clop! .... fell awkwardly ....
..... somersaulted .... crowd laughed heartily ....

A Strange Creature

Pretend you have captured one of the following imaginary folk
(leprechaun, elf, genie, pixie, nymph.)
Describe the strange creature.

Remember to tell us about its: size, appearance, dress and habits. Tell where it lives and what it
likes to eat. Perhaps the stranger has magical powers.

Helpful words.

soft music .... moonlit night .... woodland .... startled
.... spell-bound .... wrinkled face .... charms
.... tricks .... magic .... vanished.

Greece, Home Of The Olympics
Comprehension

The Olympic Games began in Greece almost three thousand years ago. The games were held every four years at Olympia in the west of Greece and were in honour of Zeus, King of the gods. When the time for the games would arrive, *heralds* were sent to every corner of the country to tell the people. Any groups at war would have to lay down their arms for a month while the games lasted. This month allowed the athletes to travel to Olympia to train for their events. A few days before the start of the games, people began to travel from all over the countryside to the great Stadium at Olympia. The valley where the games were held was a sea of little white tents as 40,000 people camped or slept out in the open. A large group of "police" armed with whips kept this big crowd well under control.

The whole of the first day was taken up with religious *ceremonies* in honour of Zeus. The opening event on the second day was the chariot race. The race was over nine kilometres and involved two-wheeled chariots drawn by teams of four horses. It was an exciting, dangerous event. In one year, forty-one chariots entered and only one finished the race. It was followed immediately by a bare back horse race over 800 metres. In the afternoon came the pentathlon which involved five events: the discus, long jump, javelin, 200 metre sprint and wrestling. Once again, the next day was taken up with religious ceremonies. The games were always fixed so that a full moon would fall on this third day. During the afternoon, one hundred cattle were *sacrificed* to please the gods. The morning of the final day saw the running of the 200 metre, 400 metre and 4,800 metre races. But the most popular events of all were the boxing and wrestling which followed in the afternoon. There were few rules, no time limit and no ring. The fights were bloody, and often ended in serious injury or even death. One winner of the boxing event was a man named Nicophon. It was written about him that "even Zeus *trembled* when he saw this giant of a man with the thick bull neck, shoulders of iron and eyes of a lion."

Although the winners did not receive any prize other than a simple olive *wreath*, they were usually richly rewarded when they returned home. A winner at Olympia received a hero's welcome. A 200 metre champion once returned to his home in Sicily and was taken around his city in a parade of three hundred chariots, each drawn by a pair of white horses!

These great games lasted for a thousand years. They eventually died out and were forgotten. When they were started again in 1896, it was fitting that the first games of modern times were held in Greece, home of the Olympics.

Dictionary work: Find out the meaning of: heralds; ceremonies; sacrificed; trembled; wreath. Write each word in a sentence of your own.

Questions

1. Where were the Olympic Games held?
2. Why did the athletes travel early to the games?
3. What did the valley at Olympia look like at the time of the games?
4. Describe the chariot race.
5. What would happen on the afternoon of the third day of the games?
6. Which were the most popular events of the Olympics?
7. What did the winners receive?
8. Write out the timetable of events for the four days of the Olympics.
9. What are the main differences between the modern Olympic Games and the Olympic Games of ancient Greece?

Question Marks

Always start a question with a capital letter and end it with a question mark(?).

Why?	**Examples:**	Why did he go there?
Where?		Where are you going?
When?		When is he coming?
What?		What are you doing?
Who?		Who is there?
Which?		Which pen is yours?
How?		How is your headache?

(A) Write out the following questions correctly, by inserting the capital letters and the question marks.

1. how old are you
2. why is the school closed today
3. where is the circus
4. who won the race
5. when is the bus coming

6. whose coat is this
7. what did she buy
8. which house is yours
9. shall we go shopping
10. is this your coat

(B) Write down questions for which the following are the answers.

1. She is twelve years of age.
2. He left the room because he was angry.
3. The train arrived at six o'clock.
4. Honeybees live in hives.
5. Tom's horse won the race.
6. The inspector came by car.
7. It is my pen.
8. The runaway horse jumped the wall.
9. Our new teacher decorated the room.
10. She decided to buy the yellow frock.

(C) Write two questions that each of the following people might ask.

1. A motorist.
2. A lost girl.
3. An American tourist visiting London.
4. A British tourist visiting America.
5. A newspaper reporter.
6. A detective
7. A hungry boy.
8. A customer in a shop.

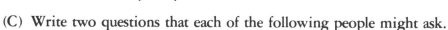

Sammy Snail
Comprehension

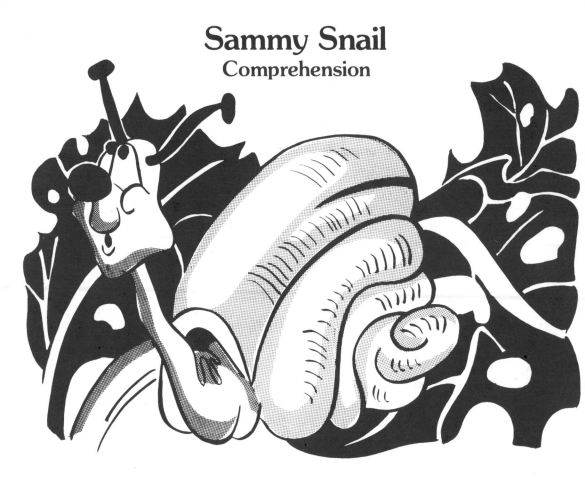

Sammy Snail is a wonderful little creature. He has no ears or nose. He lives in a spiral-shaped house called a shell. It is small in size but it widens out to form a *rim* near the mouth. He *inherited* it from his parents. As Sammy grew, so did his shell. Although he has no hands, he can carry two hundred times his own weight on his back. Imagine what would happen to you if you tried to carry two hundred times your own weight!

Though Sammy has no legs, he manages to travel about in all directions. He lays down a trail of slime to help him glide over rough and dry ground. On his head he has two pairs of feelers or tentacles. He finds his way about with the short pair of feelers. When his enemies are *approaching* he receives warning signals. He can then draw his feelers in and out as he pleases.

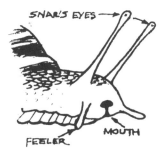

Did you know that a snail's tongue is covered with as many as twenty five thousand file-like teeth? These tiny teeth help him grind the green cabbage leaves, the young plants and the garden fruits. If you touch a snail's boneless body, he curls up and closes the mouth of his shell. He is able to do this with the aid of a sticky slime, called mucus, which he *manufactures* in his own body. He is a clever little creature and he has to protect himself with his shell from the cold weather and his many enemies.

His greatest enemy is the thrush. This clever bird has found a way to crack the snail's shell. He bangs it *repeatedly* against a hard stone until it breaks. He can then pick out the soft, juicy snail and eat it.

Next time you see a snail look carefully at its tiny eyes. When Sammy Snail loses an eye, he grows a new one. He cannot see very well with them but he can turn them around in all directions just like a *periscope* on a submarine. You and I have eyelids to protect our eyes. The snail also protects his eyes by rolling them down his hollow tentacles, where they are quite safe.

In winter Sammy goes to sleep. He can remain asleep without food for weeks. Next time you meet him, *observe* his movements and study his actions.

Dictionary work: Find out the meaning of: rim; inherit; approach; manufacture; repeatedly; periscope; observe. Write each word in a sentence of your own.

Questions

1. Where would you expect to find snails?
2. Where did the snail get his shell?
3. How can he travel over rough and dry ground?
4. What kind of food does he like to eat?
5. Why do gardeners dislike snails?
6. What enemies has he?
7. How does the little creature protect his eyes?
8. Give words to describe the movements of the snail.
9. How might a snail escape from a sealed, cardboard box?
10. Which of these soft-bodied creatures have shells?
    crab, worm, oyster, slug, periwinkle, starfish, octopus, clam, scallop, squid.
11. Explain the following phrases.
    (i) going at a snail's pace.
    (ii) to be a bookworm.
    (iii) squirming like a snail.

Exercises

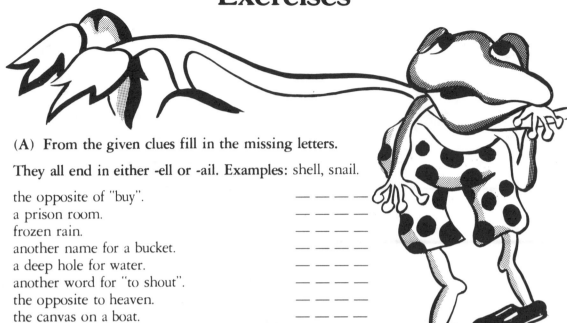

(A) From the given clues fill in the missing letters.

They all end in either -ell or -ail. Examples: shell, snail.

the opposite of "buy".   — — — —

a prison room.   — — — —

frozen rain.   — — — —

another name for a bucket.   — — — —

a deep hole for water.   — — — —

another word for "to shout".   — — — —

the opposite to heaven.   — — — —

the canvas on a boat.   — — — —

a girl's name.   — — — —

a monkey uses it for swinging.   — — — —

(B) Draw a picture of a garden snail. Write ten sentences about your picture. Tell about the snail's beautiful shell, its great strength, its colour, tiny teeth, wrinkled skin, its trail and its eating habits.

(C) Place a snail on a piece of glass. You can then study its movement as it creeps along. Do not forget to look at the flat part of its body.

(D) Write a funny story about a race between Freddy Frog and Sammy Snail.

(E) Snailery

Find a large jam-jar or an empty aquarium. Either vessel will make a good home for garden snails. Put some clean garden soil and rotting leaves or peat on the bottom of the jar or aquarium. Mix some damp chalk through the soil. The snail will use it to build up his shell. Always keep the soil damp. Keep your snailery in a cool, dark place and clean it out weekly.

(F) Imagine you are a young snail. Suddenly you see monsters such as: a horse, a frog, a dog or a cow. Write down what you thought about each one and what you told your mother when you returned home.

Size

(A) Rewrite the following in their order of size, the smallest first.

1. salmon, trout, minnow, shark.
2. alligator, frog, penguin, newt.
3. elephant, mouse, fox, rabbit.
4. duck, swan, seal, duckling.
5. zebra, monkey, kangaroo, camel.

Seasons

(B) In spring the frog lays her frog spawn in the marshes and ponds. Which season is it:

1. When the new born lambs frolic and frisk in the fields?
2. When the busy bee collects nectar from the flowers?
3. When the swallows fly away to Africa?
4. When the hedgehog goes for a long rest?
5. When the cuckoo comes to our country?
6. When the daffodils appear in the fields?
7. When the apples are picked?
8. When the wild goose arrives in our country?

(C) Write the following words in their correct places, the first one is given.

List: Friday, rough, five, flag, phone, Philip, farm, cough, fraction, flash, fun, enough, photo, freckles, flower, freeze, phrase, fork, flask, laugh, finger, flock, tough, frame, phantom, friend, father, trough, elephant, flood.

F	Fr	Fl	Ph (f sound)	....gh (f sound)
five	Friday	flag	phone	rough

Young

(D) Fill in the blank spaces with the correct word. The first one is given.

1. A caterpillar is a young butterfly or moth.
2. A fry is a young ....
3. A grub is a young ....
4. A tadpole is a young ....
5. A lamb is a young ....
6. A cygnet is a young ....
7. A kitten is a young ....
8. A calf is a young ....
9. A gosling is a young ....
10. A leveret is a young ....
11. A nestling is a young ....
12. A piglet is a young ....
13. An elver is a young ....
14. A parr is a young ....

53

The King's Problem
Comprehension

The first great scientist and inventor in history was a man named Archimedes, who was born in Sicily, around the year 285 B.C. From an early age he had a great interest in mathematics and especially liked working out sums involving very large numbers. He once even *calculated* the number of sand grains it would take to fill the whole universe! The King knew what a great *genius* Archimedes was and often turned to him for help. The king once *suspected* that a gold crown he had bought was not pure gold, but had been made from a mixture of gold and silver. However, he could not prove this because such a mixture would not affect the colour of the crown in any way. Archimedes was called in to help. For a long time he was *baffled* by the problem. Then one day it happened that he got into a bath which was full to the brim with water. When he saw how this caused the water to overflow onto the floor, Archimides knew he had solved the king's problem. In fact, so delighted was he that he jumped out of his bath, and ran into the street shouting "Eureka" (the Greek word for "I have found it"). What Archimedes had discovered was that any *object* which is put into water will raise the water by an amount exactly equal to the *bulk* of the object. All he now needed to do was place the king's crown in a jar of water and measure the increase in the level of water. Next, he put the same weight of pure gold as the crown in another jar and measured the rise in the water level. If the rise in the level of water in both jars was the same, then the king's crown was made of gold only. If the levels were different, then the crown must have been made from a mixture of gold and some other metal. It turned out that the levels were different — Archimedes had proved that the king had been cheated. And by putting weights of gold and silver into the water he was able to calculate the exact amount of the two metals in the water. Not only had Archimedes solved the king's problem, he also had made an important scientific discovery.

Dictionary work: Find out the meaning of: calculated; genius; suspected; baffled; object; bulk. Write each word in a sentence of your own.

Questions

1. Where and when was Archimedes born?
2. Why is he famous today?
3. What was the king's problem?
4. Why did he turn to Archimedes for help?
5. What happened when Archimedes got into his bath?
6. Why did he shout "Eureka!".
7. What discovery had he made.
8. What do you think the king did when it was proved he had been cheated?
9. List the names of any metals you know.
10. Write down what you know about any great inventor or scientist.

Verbs

A verb is a 'doing' or 'action' word. It is used to make a statement about a person, place or thing.

Examples: The cat **killed** the rat.
The girl **wept** bitterly.
The chair **fell** on the floor.

(A) Pick out the verbs in the following sentences.

1. House spiders weave cobwebs.
2. The squirrel built a drey.
3. The otter caught a fat waterhen.
4. The cat is purring near the fire.
5. Run before the bull charges.
6. I shall feed the robins.
7. A monkey chatters and an ape gibbers.
8. At night the owl hoots in the forest.
9. Tom will train the horse for the big race.
10. The tiger chased the wild goat.

(B) Choose a suitable verb to fill the blank spaces in the following sentences.

1. The horse .... over the fence.
2. The fox .... the goose.
3. A herd of buffaloes .... across the valley.
4. The fisherman .... a shoal of herring.
5. A frog .... bigger than a tadpole.
6. The sly fox .... from the hounds.
7. The angry bull .... at the gate.
8. A gaggle of geese .... across the road.

(C) Fill in the blank spaces with a verb opposite in meaning to the verb in bold type.

Example: Tom **lost** his wallet but his friend **found** it.

1. Peter **loved** the monkeys but Mary .... the gorillas.
2. He **sold** his old bicycle and .... a new one.
3. When the bull **appeared** at the fence the children .... quickly.
4. **Shut** the door and .... the window.
5. I **remember** people's names but I .... their addresses.
6. The elephant **raised** its leg and .... its trunk.
7. We **commenced** the exam in the morning and .... it in the afternoon.

Monsters from the Past
Comprehension

Millions and millions of years ago, giant reptiles roamed the earth. They were called **dinosaurs**, a word which means "terrible lizards". Some of these strange animals lived on land while others lived in water.

At that time the world was covered with great forests and swamps. Towering trees and *ferns*, some over 30 metres high, grew all the year round.

Just as you have changed from the time you first went to school, so too, the world has changed many times in the past. From time to time earthquakes pushed up new mountains out of the sea. Large areas of land were covered by icefields or flooded by warm seas.

When you first saw an elephant or a rhinoceros you were probably amazed by its huge size. When you are reading about dinosaurs you have to imagine creatures 3 or 4 times the size of a large elephant. Everything about these monsters of the past is big, even their names — **Tyrannosaurus, Triceratops** and **Brontosaurus**.

Let us now go back 65 million years through a time tunnel and visit the wonderful world of the dinosaurs.

Tyrannosaurus Rex — the *Tyrant* King of the lizards — is *prowling* near the edge of a big swamp. He is over seven metres high and is able to grind the thickest bones. Slowly he *swishes* his powerful tail along the ground and *lumbers* through the thick grass. This meat-eating creature has a stomach large enough to swallow a motor car. A big bull would only be a snack for him. Suddenly his wicked eyes catch sight of his enemy — the ten tonne horned Triceratops. This dragon-like monster has three horns on his head and a frilly collar around his neck.

With a *snort* and a roar the two monsters charge at each other. A terrible battle begins. Three Horns *plunges* his spear-shaped tusk into the underside of his enemy. The wounded Tyrant King roars with rage and has to fight for his life. He sinks his razor-sharp teeth deep into Three Horns' frilly collar. The two dinosaurs are locked in deadly combat. The ground trembles as once more Three Horns rushes forward. A sharp-clawed hind foot rips open his *flank*. With a last gasp, Three Horns rears up and rolls over on his back. His dying roars echo throughout the forest. The Tyrant King, with the snake-like neck, is still the champion fighter of the forest.

Dictionary work: Find out the meaning of: ferns, tyrant, prowl, swish, lumber, snort, plunge, flank. Write each word in a sentence of your own.

Questions: Answer the questions in sentence-form where possible.

1. What is the meaning of the word dinosaur?
2. When did they live on this earth?
3. Describe the world at that time.
4. Write down the names of three dinosaurs.
5. How does a dinosaur compare in size with an elephant?
6. Which one of the dinosaurs was king of the forest?
7. Who was his great enemy?
8. Where did the fight take place?
9. How did Triceratops defend himself?
10. Why do you think he lost the fight?
11. Make out a food menu that a dinosaur would enjoy.
12. Draw or paint a picture of a dinosaur that walked into your school playground. Describe him.
13. Compose a verse of poetry about a dinosaur.

A and An

Rule: In general we use "an" before words beginning with a vowel (a, e, i, o, u) and "a" before words beginning with a consonant.

Examples: a monster, an egg, a giant, an earthquake.

Some exceptions: an hour, an honest man, a university, a one-night show.

(A) Choose "A" or "An" to fill the blank spaces in the following sentences.

1. We saw .... unusual crocodile near .... marshy swamp.
2. I watched .... enormous reptile kill .... elephant in .... cave.
3. She saw .... swarm of giant ants attacking .... nest of cockroaches.
4. .... huge frog, with .... long tail, leaped into .... deep hole.
5. .... eight tonne dinosaur had .... small brain.
6. .... Iguanodon laid .... egg the size of .... football.
7. .... giant toad swallowed .... large fly.
8. .... Allosaurus was .... giant dinosaur.
9. .... Archaeopteryx was .... flying bird.
10. I sent .... old dagger to .... friend in the museum.

The Fiery Dragons

B) Finish the following story in your own words.

The old man told me that the entrance to the castle was guarded by three fiery dragons

A Helpful Vocabulary

savage jaws .... dagger-sharp teeth .... wicked, curved claws ....
thick, wrinkled skin .... blazing eyes .... flaming nostrils ....
large wings .... clumsy walk .... frilly, spiked necks ....
armour-plated tails .... roared and hissed .... escaped ....
rescued princess.

Verbs

(A) Rewrite the sentences, including the most suitable verb.

1. The busy bee *(strolled, prowled, flitted)* across the room.
2. The horrid beetle *(charged, waded, crawled)* under the stone.
3. The pretty butterfly *(hopped, hobbled, hovered)* near the rose bushes.
4. The timid snail *(flew, glided, scampered)* along the damp grass.
5. The house spider *(strode, strolled, scurried)* into its web.
6. The fat worm *(walked, waddled, wriggled)* into its burrow.
7. The prickly hedgehog *(tickled, stung, prodded)* the dog with its spines.
8. The golden eagle *(grabbed, tore, trapped)* the lamb in its talons.
9. The croaking bullfrog *(leaped, limped, flew)* into the deep pool.
10. The brown hen *(sniffed, pecked, gnawed)* the pan of oats.

(B) Fill in the missing form of the verb. (Study page 92).

Example: She **did** the test last week. She **has done** her driving test.

1. He **knew** the man. He did not .... the stranger.
2. She **wrote** a letter to her friend. She has .... to her friend.
3. He **went** for a drive. He has .... to visit his aunt.
4. He **came** late last night. I did not know if he would ....
5. He **gave** her a lovely present. He has .... her a new car.
6. The hungry dog **ate** the meat. The dog had not .... for days.
7. He **flew** to London. He had never .... by plane.
8. She **tore** up my notes. My coat was badly ....
9. The thief **hid** behind the tree. He had .... the jewels in a safe place.
10. I **forgot** the man's name. I had not .... my first meeting with him.

'Passed' is a verb. The horrid bat **passed** over my head.
'Past' is a preposition or adverb meaning: by, along, beyond or after.
The tawny owl flitted **past** my window.

(C) Write 'past' or 'passed' in the following sentences.

1. Peter saw a colony of bats as he walked .... the graveyard.
2. When the bat flew .... , Margaret screamed in terror.
3. The proud eagle swooped .... her nest.
4. Many days .... before my racing pigeon returned home.
5. They were attacked by vampire bats as they .... through the cave.
6. The loathsome bat .... on the dreaded disease, rabies.
7. At half .... eight the bus .... by my house.
8. It flew .... in wide circles and .... over the marshy swamp.
9. I .... many happy hours watching the salmon leaping over the falls.

"....ing"

Note: When a verb ends in a silent E, drop the letter E before adding ....ing.

Example: whistle, whistling.

(A) From the list of verbs, compose new words by adding .... 'ing'. Then rewrite the following sentences.

gallop, bubble, shine, croak, howl, whistle, nibble, lap, creak, blossom, crackle, clank, scream, clatter, rattle, shuffle, bray, neigh.

———————————— Cackle ———————————— Quack ————————

Example: The hens were cack**ling** and the ducks were quac**king**.

1. I saw a buck rabbit .... a juicy lettuce leaf.
2. Mary heard the bull frogs .... in the marshy pond.
3. The .... wind whistled through the keyhole.
4. The .... daffodils unfolded their golden frilly bonnets.
5. The silver grey stallion went .... across the field.
6. The .... stream gurgled over rocks and boulders.
7. The warm sun was .... brightly in the clear blue sky.
8. The .... of firewood frightened the timid squirrel.
9. The birds were .... merrily in the hedgerows and bushes.
10. The donkey was .... and the horse was ....
11. The .... waters washed the barren rocks.
12. The father oiled the .... hinges.
13. We heard the .... of chains and the .... of hooves as we passed the graveyard.
14. I was aroused by the .... of dishes and the .... of feet in the kitchen.
15. The .... seagulls glided over the waves.

Hippopotamus

The word "hippopotamus" is a Greek word which means "river horse". Everything about the animal is big, even its name. It is the second largest land animal, next to the elephant. An adult hippo weighs 3 or 4 tonnes and is about 5 metres long. It feeds only on plants. At each meal it devours about 180 kilogrammes of food. While swimming under water, the hippo closes its large nostrils and stumpy ears.

Unusual Fish

Piranha

The piranha lives in the Amazon and Orinoco Rivers of South America. It is one of the world's most vicious and dangerous fish. Although it is only about 30 cms. in length, it is afraid of neither man nor beast.

These razor-toothed fish swim in great schools and have been known to attack alligators and herds of cattle, *wading* across a stream. Within seconds they can crush and devour their victims, leaving only a bare skeleton.

Unfortunate natives and explorers have also been attacked by piranhas and instantly devoured. Scientists say that a human being has a better chance of escaping from a school of sharks than he has from a school of piranhas.

Archer Fish

This fish lives around the warm waters of the Asiatic Coast. It has a most unusual way of hunting for food. It swims near the surface of the water keeping a sharp lookout for *innocent* insects. On spying its victim it fires a *rapid* burst of water pellets from its mouth. The insect falls into the water and is quickly devoured. The fish has excellent eyesight and *seldom* misses its target. If the first shot is *inaccurate*, it *adjusts* its aim, and nearly always scores a hit the second time. It can shoot down insects within a range of one metre.

Dictionary work: Find out the meaning of: wading; unfortunate; innocent; rapid; seldom; inaccurate; adjusts. Write each word in a sentence of your own.

Questions

1. Where would you find the piranha?
2. How can such a small fish as the piranha be so dangerous?
3. What does the archer fish feed on?
4. How does it catch its victim?
5. List the names of other fish you know.
6. Can you name 5 of the world's largest rivers?
7. Write 10 sentences about any other fish.

The Snowfall
Creative Writing

Helpful words and ideas:

.... opened curtains .... delightful surprise .... thick blanket of snow .... everything hushed and still .... rows of gleaming icicles .... breakfast of piping-hot porridge .... robin huddled on window sill .... crumbs .... rushed outside .... knee deep in powdery snow .... trail of fox prints .... gently falling snow flakes .... snowman .... tossed snowballs .... best friend arrived with a sleigh. .... steep hill .... hurtling downwards .... overturned .... rolled and tumbled .... sleigh-riding all day .... trudged home .... hot dinner .... crackling log fire ....

Collective Terms

(A) Write one name for each of the following sets.

1. fir; oak; ash; chestnut; .... trees ....
2. shark; salmon; trout; plaice; ....
3. Alps; Rockies; Himalayas; Mourne; ....
4. Atlantic; Pacific; Indian; Arctic; ....
5. Japan; Ireland; Greenland; France; ....
6. New York; Moscow; Peking; Dublin; ....
7. canoe; punt; barge; catamaran; ....
8. guitar; flute; violin; mandolin; ....
9. viper; python; cobra; asp; ....
10. Pluto; Venus; Mars; Saturn; ....

(B) Make an interesting sentence with each of the following.

1. The fleet of ships ....
2. A clump of trees ....
3. The shoal of herring ....
4. The flock of sheep ....
5. A herd of buffaloes ....
6. The kennel of dogs ....
7. The Indian tribe ....
8. An army of soldiers ....
9. The class of children ....
10. A choir of angels ....

(C) Write the correct group term for each of the following (Study page 94).

1. a .... of goats	9. a .... of grapes
2. a .... of insects	10. a .... of lions
3. a .... of chickens	11. a .... of pups
4. a .... of cards	12. a .... of wolves
5. a .... of foxes	13. a .... of whales
6. a .... of bees	14. a .... of mules
7. a .... of mice	15. a .... of swallows
8. a .... of geese	16. a .... of horses

An Amazon Tribe
Comprehension

This is Dako, a young South American Indian. He is a member of the Xingu tribe and lives in the hot forests of the Amazon jungle. Their *settlement* is on the banks of the River Xingu. They chose this *site* because of the need for a regular supply of fish and fresh water. They often kill the wild animals that come to drink near the water's edge.

Dako's home was built by his father and members of the tribe. First, they cleared away a large patch of forest land with their axes. Then they cut down the tall trees, ferns and creepers. One palm tree was left standing in the centre of the clearing. Around this central pole they built a large wooden frame of bamboos. These were fastened together with string ropes made from creepers. Next, the cone-shaped hut was thatched and lined with large palm leaves and sheets of bark. The entrance was a small opening in the side of the hut. A curtain of hanging leaves covered the doorway. Inside the hut Dako's mother always kept a fire *smouldering*. The smoke helped to keep away horrid beetles, nasty flies and buzzing mosquitos.

Dako often goes on hunting expeditions with members of the tribe. The Xingus use large blow-pipes, over two metres long, to shoot small animals and birds living high up in the trees. When travelling through the jungle the *natives* feast on wild berries, honey and bananas. A hunting trip is always exciting and dangerous. The *shrieks* of parrots and toucans echo throughout the *dense* jungle. The Xingus are expert trackers. They move with care and *caution* through the forests, so as not to disturb a nest of red ants or a poisonous snake.

They fish in hollowed-out tree trunks just like the Stone Age men did thousands of years ago. Turtles and fish are harpooned with sharp, pointed spears. While fishing, there is always the danger of an alligator overturning the dug-out canoe and devouring the helpless hunters.

When the tribesmen are out hunting, the womenfolk are busy at home weaving baskets and cooking wild berries and roots. The roots of the cassava are peeled and soaked in water to remove their poison. The mashed roots are then cooked over the campfire and are enjoyed by the men when they return from the hunt.

Dictionary work: Find out the meaning of: settlement; site; smouldering; native; shriek; dense; caution.

Questions

1. Where does Dako live?
2. What is the name of his tribe?
3. Why does the tribe live near a river?
4. How was the hut built?
5. What is the purpose of the fire?
6. How are the Xingus like the Stone Age men?
7. What food do Dako and his friends eat?
8. What weapons have the Xingus?
9. How do they catch fish?
10. How is the poison extracted from the roots of the cassava?

65

Activities

1. Imagine you crashed in the Amazon Jungle. Describe your exciting survival. Perhaps you met a member of the Xingu tribe.
2. Make a booklet about interesting tribes: Australian Aborigines, Bushmen of the Kalahari Desert, Dani of New Guinea.
3. Make a model of a tribal hut like the one in the picture. You could use lollipop sticks and plasticine to cover the exterior.

Exercises

Defence and Attack

(A) From the clues given, name the creatures.
Example: I defend myself by stinging.   Honeybee ....

1. I goad and puck people with my horns.   G ....
2. I grip and pinch you with my nippers.   C ....
3. I swoop and snatch my prey with my talons.   E ....
4. I use my sharp teeth and claws to kill.   T ....
5. I hiss and frighten people with my forked tongue.   S ....
6. I attack with my strong ivory tusks.   E ....
7. I use my prickly spines to defend myself.   H ....
8. I float in the sea and sting you.   J ....
9. I live in jungle swamps and have powerful jaws and
   tail.   C ....
10. I crush my prey to death with my long, scaly body. B ..... C ....

(B) Fill in the blank spaces with a suitable word.
Example: Bee is to hive as bird is to nest.

1. Cow is to byre as horse is to ....
2. Butterfly is to caterpillar as frog is to ....
3. Beef is to cow as mutton is to ....
4. Hoof is to horse as .... is to dog.

(C) Examine the clues and insert the missing letters.
Example: Busy, buzzing insects.   BEES

1. A vehicle used by the army.   -EE-
2. A wild plant in the garden.   -EE-
3. An animal with antlers.   -EE-
4. A vegetable like an onion.   -EE-
5. The meat of a cow.   -EE-
6. To shed tears.   -EE-
7. To spy through the keyhole.   -EE-
8. Part of your foot.   -EE-
9. Another word for "humble".   -EE-
10. Used for winding thread and fishing tackle. -EE-

Story

(D) Complete the following story in your own words.

The wicked wasps annoyed and teased Danny.
Their buzzing sound filled the kitchen as they zoomed up and down the room.
"I will frighten them with my stick," thought Danny.

(E) Like and Unlike

1.	be, bee	Which is an insect?
2.	place, plaice	Which is a flat fish?
3.	flour, flower	Which grows in the garden?
4.	boar, bore	Which is a wild pig?
5.	herd, heard	Which is a collection of animals?
6.	beach, beech	Which is a tree?
7.	hair, hare	Which is a wild animal?
8.	lair, layer	Which is a fox's home?
9.	yew, ewe	Which is a female sheep?
10.	coarse, course	Which means "rough"?

'A and An'

Note: "An" is generally used before a word beginning with a vowel (a,e,i,o,u).

(F) Insert "A" or "An" in the blank spaces in the following sentences.

1. Mary saw .... owl swoop down and kill .... mouse.
2. .... eel wriggles like .... worm.
3. .... oyster lives in .... shell.
4. .... spider is not .... insect.
5. .... hyena makes .... unusual sound.
6. .... rabbit lives in .... underground home.
7. .... flat worm is usually smaller than .... earthworm.

(G) Complete the following to make interesting sentences.

1. The angry swarm of bees ....
2. She felt a sharp sting ....
3. The busy bee flew ....
4. At the end of the garden I discovered ....
5. On a recent visit to the zoo I ....
6. The explorer in the jungle ....
7. A huge, snarling dog ....
8. As soon as dawn broke ....

The Mountain Hike

Write an essay:

Helpful words and ideas.

meeting with friends .... planned route .... prepared picnic ....
arrangements ....
.... following morning .... cloudless sky of blue .... brisk pace
.... mountain path .... tall pines .... songs of larks ....
clear, crystal streams .... chatting happily ....
.... midday .... sweltering heat .... leafy shade of oak tree
.... sharing lunch .... game of hide and seek .... deep into forest
.... friend missing .... organised search party .... finally
spotted .... sighs of relief ....
.... packed bags .... cleared litter .... long road home ....
.... slept soundly.

The Queen Bee
Comprehension

The honey-bee's hive is a strange and *fascinating* place. It is ruled by the great queen bee. She is bigger and stronger than the worker or male bees in the hive. She wears a beautiful chocolate-brown dress, striped with bands of gold. Her chief duty is to lay eggs in the empty brood cells of the hive. During the breeding season the queen of the hive lays between 1,500—2,000 eggs daily.

When the queen is ready to marry, she leaves the hive and flies into the air in a *spiral* pattern. The male bees, called drones, follow her. The powerful queen flies higher and higher into the sky. Finally, she chooses the greatest and strongest drone as her husband. Shortly after the wedding flight her husband, the drone bee, dies. The royal queen, now a widow returns to the hive to begin the task of egg-laying. During the next two or three years she will lay as many as a million eggs.

On her return to the hive she is given a royal *reception*. Worker bees *escort* her round the honeybee kingdom, which is a palace of polished and varnished wax. The workers attend her majesty and feed her on a diet of royal jelly. This jelly is made in little factories at the top of their heads. It is a rich food and is necessary for the queen during her season of egg laying.

The queen lays an egg about the size of a grain of sand in each of the little brood cells. Each egg is carefully fastened to the bottom of the cell with a drop of glue from her body. It takes three days for the egg to hatch out into a hungry bee grub called larva. The nurse-bees feed it well and the tiny grub quickly swells and grows. Soon it fills up the cell. Next, a wax cap is placed over the brood cell. While the grub sleeps, curled up in a silken blanket, a strange and magical change takes place. Just three weeks after the egg was laid a young worker bee, with wings, chews its way through the cell roof and crawls out, ready to live and work in the new hive.

After two or three years the queen begins to fail at her work. Her daughters then decide to *rear* a young princess. They build large royal cells near the edge of the honeycomb. In these the queen lays eggs. The newly born babies are fed only royal jelly. In some *miraculous* way one of the tiny eggs that might have become a worker or drone bee develops into a beautiful princess. If two queens hatch out at the same time, they have a *duel* to the death, as only one queen may rule the hive.

Sometimes the hive becomes overcrowded. When this happens the old queen leaves to establish a new home. She is followed by a great swarm of bees. The beekeeper gives the colony of bees a new home. Meanwhile the bees in the old hive rear a young queen of their own.

Dictionary work: Find out the meaning of: fascinating; spiral; reception; escort; rear; miraculous; duel. Write each word in a sentence of your own.

Questions

1. Where does the queen lay her eggs?
2. What are male bees called?
3. What is the importance of "royal jelly"?
4. When do bees usually swarm?
5. Why are there nurse-bees in the hive?
6. Why is the queen so important for the survival of the hive?
7. How does the queen display her strength and superiority?
8. What happens to the queen's husband?
9. What happens when there are two queens in a hive?
10. Describe the queen bee.

Underline the correct word in brackets.

Example: a comb of honey.

a grain of *(milk, nuts, sugar)*.

a pinch of *(salt, tea, grass)*.

a morsel of *(snuff, food, pepper)*.

a pat of *(fish, butter, cheese)*.

a flake of *(sun, smoke, snow)*.

a speck of *(dirt, dye, glass)*.

a posy of *(cats, horses, flowers)*.

a crumb of *(ice, buns, bread)*.

a splinter of *(grass, glass, cloth)*.

a drop of *(coffee, water, soap)*.

Insects

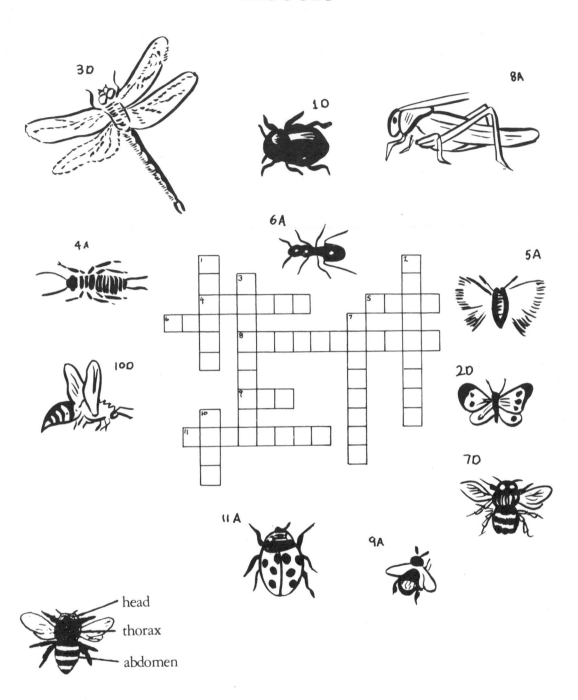

head
thorax
abdomen

Note

There are more insects in the world than there are animals. True insects have no bones but they have 6 legs and a pair of feelers. Their bodies are divided into 3 parts — head, thorax and abdomen.

More Confusing Words

(i) "**Done**" must always be used with helping words like: has, have, had, was, were, is, are.
Example: Dako's mother had **done** the washing.
(ii) "**Did**" can stand alone.
Example: Dako's mother **did** the cooking for the family.

Did and Done

(A) Insert 'did' or 'done' in the following sentences.

1. Where .... they build the hut?
2. Dako's sister .... not know if the stew was .... or not.
3. Dana .... basket weaving while Dako .... the wood carvings.
4. The work was .... but the chief .... not know who had ......
    ...... it.
5. .... the hunter kill the jaguar? Yes, he ....

Of and Off

(B) Fill in the blank spaces with either 'of' or 'off'.

1. The referee ordered the player .... the field at the end .... the game.
2. The tall runner set .... before the rest .... the field.
3. The fox ran .... with two .... mother's hens.
4. The man took .... his coat and jumped .... the rock.
5. Joan, the baby .... the family, was afraid .... the big dog next door.
6. Angela turned .... the television set before going .... to bed.
7. The two .... them strolled .... down the dusty road.
8. At the far end .... the field the player was carried .... on a stretcher.
9. Which .... you tore .... the new cover .... my book?
10. He was so well .... that he gave much .... his money to charitable
    organisations.

There and Their

(C) Fill in the blank spaces with either 'there' or 'their'.

1. The swallows were .... with .... friends the house martins.
2. Some birds obtain .... food by digging with .... bills.
3. To .... amazement the penguins fluttered .... wings and waddled towards
    ...... camera.
4. The killer whales seized .... victims in .... jaws and disappeared.
5. .... is a kingfisher on that rock over ....
6. .... were hundreds of crows flying home to .... nests in the wood.
7. The barn swallows built .... nests .... last year.
8. Scientists came to .... village to study .... habits and customs.

73

The Garden Spider
Comprehension

The garden spider is a funny little creature. On her back is a stripe in the shape of a cross. Perhaps this is the reason she is called the Cross Spider. She has the most beautiful pointed claws at the tip of each of her eight hairy legs. With these claws she combs and *trims* herself. Her many legs help her travel quickly. At the first sign of danger she *scurries* into the safety of her web. Did you know that on top of her head she has eight tiny sparkling eyes which help her see in different directions.

If you examine the garden spider through a magnifying glass, you will notice that she has a tiny mouth. In front of it are two poisonous *fangs*, which she can fold over her lips like the blades of a penknife. With these she injects poison into the flies and insects that she traps in her web.

We eat with our hands but the spider uses a pair of hooked feelers called "palps". She likes to nibble the soft insides of her victims. The next time you see a spider's web, look carefully at the empty *carcasses* lying around the web.

When it comes to housekeeping, few can compete with the spider. Before the sun peeps over the mountain tops she begins to spin her web. Sometimes she works throughout the night, weaving and spinning it into shape, in order to *snare* the early morning gnats and flies. She is well equipped for her work. In her body are six spinning fingers called "spinnerets". From these come thin silken threads which harden as soon as they meet the air. These slender elastic-type threads are carefully woven back and forth to form a beautiful crochet of webs. Some of the threads are coated with sticky *beads* of glue which help to trap and capture the careless flies and insects. Her feet are covered with an oily substance that helps her glide over these sticky threads. Mrs. Spider must feel very proud when she gazes on her web of pearls *glistening* in the early morning mist.

Dictionary work: Find out the meaning of: trim; scurry; fang; carcasses; snare; bead; glisten. Write each word in a sentence of your own.

Questions

1. What is the spider's favourite food?
2. How does she gather it?
3. Why is the garden spider's web sticky?
4. How does she avoid being trapped?
5. Write out words with the same meaning as: tiny, beautiful, sparkling.
6. What are 'palps'?
7. How is she able to travel about quickly?
8. Write the following words in sentences.
   palps, spinnerets, claws, gnats.
9. Describe briefly and clearly how the garden spider's web is made.

   Here are some words to help you.

   frame of strong threads .... firmly secured .... scaffolding .... strands of fine silk thread .... fastens sticky beads .... circular patterns .... shaped like the spokes of a wheel .... a slender signal-line from the centre of the web to a hiding place.
10. Where in the garden would you expect to find a spider's web?
11. Imagine you are a house spider.

Complete the following story. The first paragraph is written.

All day I hid in a dark corner of the kitchen. That night when the house was quiet and everyone was asleep, I ventured out. Silently I began to spin my web. Although I had neither candle nor lamp, my eyes helped me work in the dark.

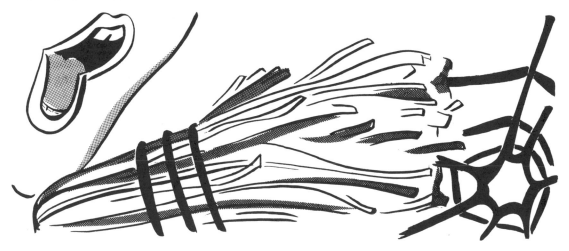

Helpful words and phrases.

spun thin threads .... fine close-meshed web .... trap for flies and moths .... sat in a little tunnel of silk .... waited and watched .... discovered .... angry housewife .... big broom .... swept .... narrowly escaped death .... scurried to safety .... hid behind the cupboard.

75

(A) House Spider

This spider spins a close-meshed web, called a cobweb. The crochet of webs is not the least bit sticky. The web is usually found in a corner between walls or presses. The spider's living room is in a dark silken tube at the topmost corner of the web.

(B) Zebra Spider

The zebra spider is a pretty little creature. On sunny evenings it likes to go hunting flies. This spider pounces on its prey, just like a cat *stalks* a bird. It creeps up silently on the fly. Now and again it freezes and pretends to be dead. Suddenly the spider springs on the fly, digs in its poisonous fangs and has a delicious meal.

(C) Crab Spider

This spider moves like a crab. The hairy *pads* on its feet help it walk up a *glossy* leaf. It does not snare insects in a web, but it has many tricks to capture them. The crab spider is unusual in the way it can change colour. There is one species that can change colour from yellow to white and back again to yellow so as to *blend* with the surrounding flowers. The male spider wears a pretty yellow striped-dress as a disguise. It sits quietly in the heart of a yellow flower, waiting to pounce on an insect that may come to drink a dewdrop.

(D) Wolf Spider

The wolf spider lives among the stones and the grass. It builds no web and it has no *permanent* home. It wanders and hunts its prey like the hungry wolf. Perhaps the most startling thing about this spider is the way the mother cares for her young. She lays 50 to 100 eggs in a tiny silken sheet. This is wrapped up and carried like a bag under the spider's body. Attached to her spinnerets, it looks like a tiny white ball. When the young spiders hatch out, they climb on to the mother's back and cling to her hairy body. During the winter the mother and her babies sleep in a nook or cranny. The following spring the babies venture into the nearby woods and grasses and begin a new life.

(E) Garden Spider

In autumn the female garden spider builds a soft cradle of silk for her family. It is shaped like a blackbird's egg. She lays hundreds of eggs inside the silken cocoon. This is hidden among the leaves or *crevices* under the window-ledges and doors. Alas! the mother spider, weary and tired, has no energy left to spin her own web. During the cold and frosty weather her body shrinks and she dies. Poor Mrs. Spider does not live to see her new-born family.

In spring the young spiders hatch out and spin their first threads by which they can travel from the cocoon to the ground. Soon the spiderlings moult or shed their outer skins. Now they can grow bigger as their new skin is soft and delicate.

On a calm, spring morning, the spiderlings climb to the top of a branch or bush. Standing on tip-toe they cast out streamers of silk, which waft and float in the gentle breeze. We call these "gossamer threads". Perhaps you have felt these "gossamer threads" tickle your face as you hurried to school. The threads travel upwards and carry the attached spiders to new homes. When they come to rest, the spiderlings *discard* their silken parachutes.

Although they have never seen or made a web, presently the spiderlings will spin perfect webs, just like their parents. Mrs. Spider is one of nature's greatest engineers and architects.

(F) Black Widow Spider

Almost all spiders are harmless but a few species have a strong poison. One of these is the Black Widow. It is one of the most poisonous of all spiders. It got its name from the female member of the family. On the underside of her shiny black body are red markings. She is more than twice the size of the male spider and after mating she often devours her husband and is then a widow. Indeed some form of *cannibalism* is common enough among most spiders. The Black Widow is found in the warm regions of South and Central America.

(G) Look and Learn

A few house spiders can be studied in captivity. A large glass or plastic jar will make a suitable home for the spiders. Place a small piece of moist flannel in the bottom of the jar. Next put a little crumpled paper or bare twig in each jar, and sprinkle with water. This acts as a frame for the spider's cobweb.

Place only one house spider in each jar, as spiders eat each other *(are cannibals)*. House spiders must be fed with live flies. They need plenty of food to help them have material for spinning webs. In spring the big female spider can be watched as she spins her cocoon. Later, the young spiders hatch out.

Keep nature notes of the things you notice from day to day. Treat the spiders gently and with kindness. Do not keep them too long in captivity.

Dictionary work: Find out the meaning of: stalks; pads; glossy; blend; cannibalism. Write each word in a sentence of your own.

Questions

1. Which spider can change its colour.
2. Which spider takes good care of its young?
3. Which spider often devours its husband?
4. Which spider spins a cobweb?
5. Which spider creeps up silently on its victim?
6. Which spider dies after laying its eggs?
7. Spiders are essential to life on earth. Can you guess why?

Homonyms

Homonyms are words pronounced alike but different in spelling and meaning.

(A) Choose the correct homonym to fill the blank spaces.

1. Seven days(week)
   Feeble ... (weak)
2. Sixty minutes ..
   Belonging to us
3. Expensive ......
   An animal ......
4. Shines in sky ...
   A male child ...

5. Quietness .....
   A part ....
6. To pull ....
   Of the foot ...
7. Of a ship ......
   To sell ....
8. A story ....
   Part of a dog .

9. Useless ....
   Part of the body
10. A strand ......
    Type of tree ..
11. An animal ....
    Of the head ...
12. Verb 'to hear' .
    A group of
    animals ....

13. Verb 'to know'
    Not used before
14. To use a needle
    To place seeds .
15. Of glass ....
    Ache ....
16. For a lock ......
    A dock ....

(B) Choose the correct word from those in the margin to fill the blank spaces.

ate, eight:
hole, whole:
berry, bury:
our, hour:
new, knew:
red, read:
nose, knows:
yew, ewe:
would, wood:
threw, through:
quiet, quite:
won, one:
fair, fare:

1. It was ..... o'clock before I ..... a morsel of food.
2. He hid the ..... amount of his savings in a deep .....
3. When you ..... that red ..... it will grow into a tree.
4. It was an ..... later that ..... boat departed from the quay.
5. Everyone ..... that he bought a ..... bicycle.
6. She ..... the title on the cover of the ..... book.
7. The trainer ..... that the player's ..... is fractured.
8. The ram and the ..... stood near the ..... tree.
9. Harry ..... like to go for a nature walk through the .....
10. She ..... the ball ..... the window.
11. He was ..... right. The place was very ....
12. Which ..... of you ..... the race?
13. The .... haired man thought the ..... on the bus was very dear.

(C) Which is which?

1. Grate, great.   Which is a fireplace? ....
2. Teem, team.   Which is a group of people? ....
3. Pair, pear, pare. Which is a fruit? ....
4. Leek, leak.   Which is a vegetable? ....
5. Bow, bough.   Which is a branch? ....

Words and Nature

(A) Write the correct name of each creature in the blank space. The first one is given. (Study page 93).

1. The **bee** hums.
2. The .... bleats.
3. The .... neighs.
4. The .... brays.
5. The .... barks.
6. The .... roars.
7. The .... chatters.
8. The .... growls.
9. The .... gibbers.
10. The .... purrs.
11. The .... lows.
12. The .... bellows.
13. The .... quacks.
14. The .... cackles.
15. The .... squeaks.
16. The .... croaks.
17. The .... whistles.
18. The .... squeals.
19. The .... coos.
20. The .... chirps.

(B) Fill in the blank spaces. (Study page 94).

1. I awoke the .... day as fresh as a ....
2. The table he .... was as sturdy as an ....
3. He .... the race because he ran as fast as a ....
4. Her hair was as black as .... and her skin was as white as ....
5. The gymnast on the .... was as agile as a ....
6. I will be as busy as an .... for the rest of the ....
7. After winning the .... she was as .... as a lark.
8. The old man of the .... was as wise as an ....
9. Anyone who .... the earth is flat is as mad as a ....
10. If you keep eating all that .... you will be as fat as a ....

(C) Write the following three words in an interesting sentence.
Example: (rabbit; dashed; timid) The timid rabbit dashed for the safety of his burrow .

1. roared; lion; fierce;
2. lamb; frisky; hopped;
3. bounded; deer; swift;
4. swan; graceful; glided;
5. howled; wolf; hungry;
6. gorilla; hairy; leapt;
7. climbed, kitten; playful;
8. squirrel; scampered; agile;

The Mute Swan
Comprehension

The *mute* swan is our largest bird. She lives all the year round on our rivers, lakes and ponds. Her sail-like wings and broad webbed feet help her to glide gracefully along our waterways. She is a silent bird but when *aroused* is dangerous and makes a hissing noise.

The adult swan wears a beautiful snow-white dress. She has a black knob at the base of her bright orange-coloured bill. Her long curved neck enables her to reach down into the water and pluck up weeds and grasses. She enjoys a tasty meal of eel-grass and water insects, at the water's edge. Her *sieve*-like yellow bill has tiny grooves which help her to *sift* her food.

Once airborne, the mute swan is a powerful flier. It is hard to believe that this bird, weighing about 12 kilograms, can cruise along at speeds of 60-80 kilometres per hour. While in flight she utters a deep musical sound and you can hear the whistling of her wings as she passes overhead.

This large white bird is a devoted wife and mother. Her husband helps her to build the nest at the water's edge. He carries reeds, weeds and grasses to his partner. With these materials she builds the nest.

During the breeding season the female swan, called a **pen**, lays 4-10 greenish-white eggs. Both birds take turns at hatching the eggs. Before sitting on the eggs, the swan carefully *preens* and dries her feathers in order to keep the eggs warm. The male swan, called a **cob**, guards them from thieving rats and hungry otters. Those who *venture* too near the nest risk being attacked by an angry swan. A blow from a swan's powerful wings is capable of injuring or breaking a person's arm.

At birth the young swans or cygnets are a rusty brown colour. Within a few days they are brought sightseeing and swimming along the river, on their proud parents' backs. After a few months they leave home to begin their new lives. It takes about 3 years for cygnets to grow and develop into beautiful adult swans.

Dictionary work: Find out the meaning of: mute, aroused, sieve, preens, venture, sift. Write each word in a sentence of your own.

Questions: Answer the questions in sentence-form where possible.

1. Where do you usually see mute swans?
2. What use does she make of her webbed feet?
3. How does she find her food?
4. Is the swan a good flier?
5. What special name has each parent?
6. What materials do the parents use to build their nest?
7. Why does the swan dry her feathers before sitting on the eggs?
8. What enemies has the swan?
9. What are young swans called?
10. How do they go sightseeing?
11. When do cygnets become adult swans?
12. Draw a picture of a swan and her cygnets.
13. Write a verse of poetry about the swan.

The Whooper Swan

The whooper swan is one of our winter visitors from Iceland. It announces its arrival with a loud bugle-call. While swimming, this great white bird holds its long neck up straight. Unlike the mute swan, its wing feathers are not raised. When migrating, whooper swans fly in a straight line or trail in a V-shaped pattern.

The Desert Trek

Write a story about an expedition into the desert to search for the ruins of a lost city.

Helpful words and ideas.

.... dusty town .... bought supplies .... camels ....
set out .... desert track .... the sun beating down ....
a vast wilderness .... camped .... freezing, night air ....
continued our journey .... miles of sand-dunes .... tired and weary ....
thirsty and hungry .... came to an oasis* .... a fresh spring of clear water ......
..... cool palm trees .... desert fruits .... a welcome rest ......
..... trudged onwards .... a great discovery .... buried under sand ......
.... fallen walls .... broken statues .... began to dig ....
.. precious beads .... gold coins .... the journey homewards ....

*An Oasis is a spot in the desert where water is found and grass, trees etc. can grow.

Quotation Marks

Examples: (i) "I wish we could go swimming today", says Fiona.

(ii) Sharon says, "She is a fine dancer".

(iii) "Where will we leave the bicycles?" asked Fiona.

When writing the above sentences, only the words spoken are written inside the quotation marks.

(A) Write out the following sentences correctly. Where needed put in the quotation marks, commas and question marks.

1. Paul has ruined my painting sobbed Lorraine.
2. Did you hear about the flood in Main Street asked Neil.
3. I sentence you to a month in prison said the judge.
4. Once upon a time there was a small cottage in the woods whispered the storyteller.
5. The huntsman roared The Fox is making for the woods.
6. Kevin promised I will return your books on Friday.
7. Nora wished I hope granny brings one of her chocolate cakes.
8. I know nothing about the stolen watch lied Conor.
9. Do not stray from the forest path warned Little Red Riding Hood's grandmother.
10. The captain urged We must try harder in the second half.

(B) Rewrite the following paragraph inserting capital letters, full stops and quotation marks where necessary.

yesterday pedro and isabella had great fun in the orange grove the day was sunny and warm and suitable for orange picking isabella enjoyed picking the fruit she wore gloves to save the skin of the oranges being spoilt her brother pedro climbed the ladder and picked oranges from the top of the tree just imagine isabella said pedro this orange I'm eating may be eaten by an irish boy at noon their father arrived in a truck to collect the fruit he was very pleased with their work they quickly loaded the fruit onto the truck their father allowed them to travel with him to the market in madrid as they sped along the dusty road towards the big city he turned to them and said next sunday i will bring the pair of you to see the great carlos fight the bulls in valencia.

Creatures of the Night

Bats belong to the family of mammals. Mammals are warm-blooded animals and their babies are born alive and not hatched from an egg. Dogs, cats and elephants are other members of the same family. The bat is the only mammal that can really fly. Others, like the "flying squirrel", merely glide through the air.

A young bat, when born, lives in a little pouch that its mother makes by bending her tail forward. Later, it clings to its mother's fur with its sharp claws and teeth. It can enjoy riding with her through the air. After a few days the baby is left at home while the mother goes hunting for food. Sometimes she will catch enough insects in an hour to last a few days. After a **few weeks** the young bat is strong enough to fly and hunt for insects.

While *flitting* through the air the bat catches the insects in its mouth. Some bats trap tiny insects in their wide wings. Beetles, moths and spiders are stored in the *mesh* of skin spanning the bat's tail. In tropical lands there are large bats called "flying foxes", with a wing-span of two metres. Their heads look like those of tiny foxes. These bats *gorge* themselves on fruit, especially bananas.

Bats have poor eyesight but have a marvellous echo system to guide them through pitch darkness. While flying, the featherless bat sends out loud twittering squeaks. These squeaks bounce off nearby objects and make an echo. The bat's keen sense of hearing picks up the warning echo. In this way it flies skilfully around the object and avoids crashing into it. The bat's hearing or sonar system helps it *navigate* through dark caves and dense forests. Also it guides it towards flying insects. You and I cannot hear the echoes or the chirping cries of the bat. Our ears are not delicate or *sensitive* enough to hear the high-pitched sounds. Scientists have discovered that bats can find their way in the dark if blindfolded. However, they are helpless if their mouths and ears are covered.

During the cold winter months bats hibernate. Often twenty or thirty of them *roost* together in some old castle, cave, mine shaft or empty dwelling. While fast asleep the bats hang head downwards from the roof of their homes. They wrap their wings around their bodies like a scarf. If they are disturbed or alarmed during the night they simply drop into the air and fly away.

Dictionary work: Find out the meaning of: discard; flitting; mesh; gorge; navigate; sensitive; roost. Write each word in a sentence of your own.

Notes

(A) The Pipistrelle Bat

The pipistrelle is one of the most common bats in these islands. It has a tiny body like that of a mouse. Its thin silky wings are joined to the rest of its body by a web of silk. While asleep it hangs head downwards by its long hooked claws. The clumsy bat uses these nails to drag itself along the ground and crawl up a fence. It has broad triangular ears to help it pick up echo sounds and avoid colliding with objects. The bat's tail is used to guide it through the air. If it wishes to stop or turn it simply bends its tail downwards like a brake.

(B) The Long-Eared Bat

This bat has a pair of ears almost as long as its body. Inside its long narrow ear is a smaller earlet. The spear-shaped earlet helps the bat to pick up echoes from both sides.

(C) The Horseshoe Bat

It has a very funny snout. Many bats send out squeaks through their mouths but this bat squeaks through its nostrils.

Questions

1. What is a mammal?
2. What do bats like to eat?
3. How do they navigate in pitch darkness?
4. How do bats capture their food?
5. What is peculair about the horseshoe bat?
6. Where would you expect to find a colony of bats?
7. Why does a bat hang upside down?
8. Describe the pipistrelle.

Adverbs

Adverbs are words which tell us more about a verb. Most adverbs are formed by adding -ly to adjectives.

(A) Change the adjectives to adverbs in these sentences.

1. He *quick* swam the first length of the pool.
2. She argued *bitter* with her mother.
3. The sun shone *brilliant* over the crowded stadium.
4. The actress spoke *calm* and *slow*.
5. He won *superb*.
6. She *brave* rescued the drowning puppy.
7. The captain spoke *quiet* to his team.
8. The garda eyed the man *suspicious*.
9. We sat *patient* in the waiting room.
10. The king ruled his kingdom *wise*.

(B) Change these adjectives to adverbs by adding -ily.

1. The bored child yawned *lazy*.
2. The footballer fell *heavy* on his shoulder.
3. The bee works *busy* from dawn to dusk.
4. The train rumbled *noisy* towards the city.
5. The baby gurgled *happy* in the cot.
6. Santa Claus chuckled *merry* to himself.
7. We returned to the haunted castle and entered *wary*.
8. The bull looked *angry* at the matador.
9. The level of the water rose *steady*.
10. The impatient businessman left *hasty*.

If the adjective ends in -y, you must change the -y to -ily in order to form the adverb.

The Swallow
Comprehension

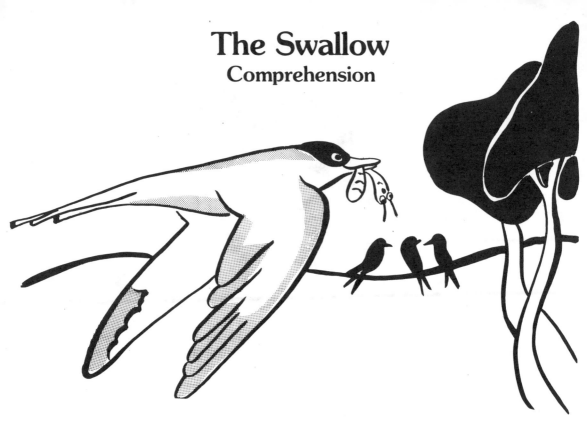

On a summer's evening you can see the flocks of twittering swallows perched on telegraph wires or flying high in the clear blue sky. They are a pretty sight to watch as they dip and dart through the air. How they love to skim over the surface of the ponds, lakes and rivers in search of insects.

The swallows build their nests inside barns, sheds and stables. The nest has no roof and is placed on a timber rafter or beam. It is made of *moist* mud, soft grasses and straws cemented together into a mud-like saucer. A soft lining of feathers keeps the nest warm and cosy. Both the parents help in the building of the *compact* nest. Their wide bills allow them scoop up clay from a nearby brook or pool. Now you know why swallows choose to live and breed near water.

The hen swallow lays four or five eggs, *blotched* and spotted with grey and orange-brown freckles. During the breeding season she may rear two or even three families. When the eggs are hatched the parents teach the young fledglings to fly and catch *gnats* and flies on the wing.

The barn swallow is easily *distinguished* by his long, deeply-forked tail, powerful strong wings and rather weak legs. They do not need to be strong like his tireless wings. His thin feet are well suited for perching on the telegraph wires. His wide beak enables him to catch insects. While skimming through the air, he opens his gaping bill and snaps up the flies and gnats. It is fun to watch this skilful bird swoop low over a lake or river and drink a droplet of water without ever touching the water with either his wings or tail.

The barn swallow wears a steel-blue *mantle* of shining feathers. He has a whitish-buff breast and a chestnut brown forehead and throat. His narrow pointed wings *taper* towards the end and are well suited for flying swiftly through the air. His v-shaped tail helps him twist and turn while in flight.

When the grey, autumn evenings grow cold and chilly, the restless swallows feel hungry. There are few insects to be found. Their cousins, the house-martins, join them on the roof-tops and telegraph wires, twittering excitedly. They seem to whisper to each other, "Insects are few. Let us fly to warmer lands". They are mysteriously *beckoned* towards Africa's sunny coasts. They travel over land and sea, mountains and valleys before they reach their destination. Once there, they can enjoy the warm weather and the feast of insects and gnats.

Scientists and ornithologists *(people who study bird life)*, do not yet know for certain how these birds, flying without a map or a compass, reach their destination. Many people think that they depend on the sun and stars to guide them. If this is true, it would seem that birds are much cleverer than we suspected.

The following year our summer visitors return to the land of their birth. Often they will use the old nest to hatch a new clutch of eggs.

Dictionary work: Find out the meaning of: moist; compact; blotched; distinguish; mantle; taper; beckon; gnat.

Questions

1. Describe how the swallow builds its nest.
2. How does the swallow catch flies and gnats?
3. Why do swallows fly to Africa?
4. Can you explain what "Migration" means?

(i) A kingfisher builds its nest at the end of a long tunnel under the river bank.

Where do the following birds usually build their nests?

(i) sand-martin (ii) swallow (iii) owl (iv) snipe (v) eagle (vi) seagull (vii) woodpecker (viii) magpie.

(ii) Write the following list of words in alphabetical order.
swift, skylark, starling, sandpiper, swallow, seagull, swan, sparrow.

(iii) How do you think these birds got their names?

the sandpiper, the kingfisher, the skylark, the wagtail, the swift, the humming bird, the nightingale, the woodpecker, the lapwing, the dipper, the crow.

Our Feathered Friends

Plural of Nouns

General Rules for the Formation of the Plural of Nouns

Examples

1.	Most nouns simply add -S to the singular.	pen	pens
2.	Nouns ending in: -S, -X, -SH, -CH, -SS form their plural by adding -ES to the singular.	glass church box brush	glasses churches boxes brushes
3.	Nouns ending: -F or -FE in general change the -F or -FE or -V and add -ES.	loaf knife **Exceptions** roof **also:** cliff, chief, safe, dwarf, gulf, cuff, reef, proof.	loaves knives roofs
4.	Nouns ending in: -Y preceded by a consonant, change the -Y to -I and add -ES. Otherwise add -S.	lady baby **but:** boy	ladies babies boys
5.	A small number of nouns remain unchanged in the singular and plural	sheep **List:** salmon, deer, cod, snipe, plaice, trout, mackerel, spawn, grouse.	sheep
6.	Some nouns ending in: -O add -ES in the plural, others add -S. There is no simple rule. Learn each new word.	potato piano	potatoes pianos
7.	Some nouns have no singular.	**List:** suds, shears, tongs, scissors, trousers, pants, measles, thanks, tweezers, pincers, pliers.	
8.	A few nouns form their plurals by changing their middle letters.	man foot tooth	men feet teeth

91

Important Verbs

Present	Past	Past Participle
am	was	been
awake	awoke	awakened
arise	arose	arisen
beat	beat	beaten
buy	bought	bought
blow	blew	blown
begin	began	begun
bite	bit	bitten
build	built	built
creep	crept	crept
choose	chose	chosen
come	came	come
do	did	done
draw	drew	drawn
drink	drank	drunk
drive	drove	driven
eat	ate	eaten
fall	fell	fallen
fight	fought	fought
fly	flew	flown
forget	forgot	forgotten
give	gave	given
go	went	gone
grow	grew	grown
hold	held	held
hide	hid	hidden
know	knew	known
ring	rang	rung
ride	rode	ridden
rise	rose	risen
shake	shook	shaken
sing	sang	sung
speak	spoke	spoken
stand	stood	stood
steal	stole	stolen
swim	swam	swum
take	took	taken
tear	tore	torn
write	wrote	written

A Treasury of Words and Phrases

Descriptive Sounds

the babble of a stream
the blare of a trumpet
the beat of a drum
the blast of an explosion
the babbling of water
the boom of a gun
the chug of an engine
the clang of a bell
the clatter of hooves
the crack of a whip
the creak of a hinge
the crinkle of paper
the chime of a clock
the clink of a coin
the gurgle of a drain-pipe
the grinding of brakes
the hissing of steam
the hoot of a horn
the hubbub of voices
the jingle of coins
the lapping of water
the pitter-patter of raindrops
the ping of a bullet
the popping of corks
the rattle of dishes
the rasp of a file
the rumble of a train
the rush of feet
the rustling of leaves
the screech of brakes
the sighing of the wind
the swish of skirts
the sizzling of sausages
the shuffling of feet
the tramp of feet
the tick of a clock
the twang of a bow
the thunder of hooves
the wail of a siren
the whirring of wings

Sounds and Movements of Birds

the crow caws and flaps her wings
the eagle screams and swoops
the hen cackles and struts
the lark sings and soars
the owl hoots and flits
the parrot screeches and flits
the pigeon coos and flutters
the seagull screams and glides
the sparrow chirps and hops
the swallow twitters and dives
the turkey gobbles and struts
the robin chirps and hops
the duck quacks and waddles
the wren warbles and hops

Sounds and Movements of Domestic Animals

the horse neighs and gallops
the lamb bleats and frisks
the pig grunts and trots
the dog barks and runs
the cow lows and wanders
the cat purrs and steals
the bull bellows and charges
the donkey brays and jogs

Sounds and Movements of Wild Animals

the lion roars and prowls
the bear growls and lumbers
the elephant trumpets and ambles
the hyena screams and prowls
the monkey chatters and climbs
the rabbit squeals and leaps
the wolf howls and lopes
the mouse squeaks and scampers
the gorilla gibbers and swings

Collective Words

a brood of chickens
a gaggle of geese
a flock of geese
a paddling of ducks
a herd of cattle
a herd of antelope
a flock of birds
a flock of sheep
a swarm of bees
a swarm of insects
a hive of bees
a team of horses
a string of horses
a team of oxen
a troop of lions
a troop of monkeys
a herd of buffaloes
a nest of rabbits
a nest of mice
a pack of hounds
a pack of wolves
a down of hares
a fall of woodcock
a plague of locusts
a kennel of dogs
a herd of elephants
a wisp of snipe
a flight of doves
a plague of insects
a shoal of herring
a school of whales
a tribe of goats
a sloth of bears
a skulk of foxes
a pride of lions
a flight of swallows
a barren of mules
a covey of grouse
a litter of pups
a litter of cubs
a flock of geese

Similes

as sly as a fox
as tender as a chicken
as slow as a tortoise
as slow as a snail
as meek as a lamb
as brave as a lion
as proud as a peacock
as busy as a bee
as busy as an ant
as blind as a bat
as playful as a kitten
as red as a turkey-cock
as fat as a pig
as strong as a horse
as strong as an ox
as happy as a lark
as mad as a March hare
as wise as an owl
as swift as a deer
as gentle as a lamb
as frisky as a lamb
as fierce as a lion
as slippery as an eel
as agile as a monkey
as hungry as a wolf
as graceful as a swan
as obstinate as a mule
as stubborn as a mule
as timid as a rabbit
as hairy as a gorilla
as sure-footed as a goat
as silly as a sheep
as fast as a hare
as brown as a berry
as sweet as honey
as white as snow
as fresh as a daisy
as purple as the heather
as green as grass
as sturdy as an oak
as cold as ice

Masculine and Feminine Nouns

prince	princess	giant	giantess
king	queen	brave	squaw
earl	countess	mayor	mayoress
emperor	empress	instructor	instructress
host	hostess	grandfather	grandmother
duke	duchess	manservant	maidservant
count	countess	postman	postwoman
baron	baroness	author	authoress
peer	peeress	heir	heiress
prophet	prophetess	traitor	traitress
wizard	witch	enchanter	enchantress
father	mother	deacon	deaconess
hero	heroine	beau	belle
husband	wife	shepherd	shepherdess
lad	lass	tailor	tailoress
gentleman	lady	warder	wardress
brother	sister		
tutor	governess	**Animals**	
lord	lady	colt	filly
master	mistress	buck-rabbit	doe-rabbit
nephew	niece	bull	cow
son	daughter	Jack-ass	Jenny-ass
sir	madam	gander	goose
man	woman	steer	heifer
landlord	landlady	dog	bitch
headmaster	headmistress	boar	sow
bridegroom	bride	cock	hen
bachelor	spinster	stag	hind
widower	widow	fox	vixen
actor	actress	ram	ewe
abbot	abbess	Billy-goat	Nanny-goat
monk	nun	cock-sparrow	hen-sparrow
priest	priestess	bullock	heifer
waiter	waitress	tiger	tigress
manager	manageress	lion	lioness
negro	negress	bull seal	cow seal
poet	poetess	leopard	leopardess
god	goddess	Tom-cat	Tabby-cat
step-father	step-mother	he-wolf	she-wolf
steward	stewardess	drake	duck
		stallion	mare